PUMP JACKS, ROUGHNECKS, & ROUSTABOUTS

JOHN J. SCHUELKE

Thank you to all the hard-working men and women who help meet the demand for oil and gas. The industry is risky, but also rewarding. The people are what make the industry function – whether you are new or the "salty dog" on the crew, you are part of the family. We look out for each other, share our aspirations, goals, and dreams, along with the heartaches and pains.
I was proud to be part of the "oilfield family" for several decades and proud of my brothers and sisters in the industry.
Thank you to all who have shared your stories or have been a part of one of mine.

DISCLAIMER

Some of the stories contained here are based on actual events. The names have been changed to protect identities and the companies they worked for. Some of the stories have been embellished to fill in gaps and make the stories more interesting.

Recollections of events were not validated but have been taken at face value – they may not be 100% accurate, or TRUE!

johnjschuelke.com

CONTENTS

FOREWORD

Maybe you have worked in the oilfield or know someone who works in the oilfield or will one day work in the oilfield. Although it is a huge industry, the people are what make it a great career. The stories in this compilation vary from heartwarming to heartbreaking, unbelievable to humorous, myth to based-on-actual-events, and are our way of sharing what it's like to work in the oilfield.

CHAPTER ONE

THE BLUE BICYCLE HELMET WANDERER

The Yellow Cab pulled up outside the terminal at the Ted Stevens International Airport in Anchorage, Alaska. After paying the fare, Bob opened the door and banged his head on the door jamb, but, thankfully, he was wearing his blue bicycle helmet, thus preventing any injury.

After a brisk walk from the cab to the terminal in the -20°F temperature, he adjusted his backpack, which contained all his worldly possessions. A quick look around the terminal and he found the ticket counter for the oil-company-owned and -operated airline. He paid little attention to the rough and tumble looking crowd that seemed to be in awe of his beautiful blue helmet. He did chuckle to himself at a couple of cowboys wearing their 10-gallon hats and cowboy boots. How odd, he thought. Don't they know there are no cows or horses where we are going?

"Would you like to check your bag sir?" the ticket agent asked.

He chuckled. "No thank you. This bag never leaves my possession. It has everything I own."

She blushed slightly and politely said, “I have to ask. Would you like an aisle, middle, or window seat sir?”

He was quick to state, “Aisle at the front of the plane please. That way if I have to make a quick exit, it will be easier.”

Bob wandered, looking for the security entrance into the terminal. After finding the line to participate in the screening activities, he waited for what seemed like an eternity. Stripping down to the bare essentials of jeans, t-shirt, and socks, he entered the body scanner.

“Excuse me, sir. You will have to remove your headgear.”

Bob thought to himself, “Not my beautiful blue bicycle helmet.”

“Sir, please remove your headgear and place it on the belt.”

With a disgusted hmmmph, he removed the helmet and placed it on the belt for scanning. He thought, “If they damage my stuff, there is going to be hell to pay!”

He was released to gather his belongings and quickly scrambled to collect his blue helmet. Once his possessions were his again, he hoisted his backpack onto his back, strapped on his helmet, and wandered through the terminal to find food.

The eggs were runny, the toast burned, and the bacon barely cooked, but it filled the empty void in his stomach. Bob was temporarily satiated and ready for his flight to the frozen North Slope.

Thirty minutes prior to boarding the plane, he waited anxiously in line. Backpack, check; helmet, check. He was prepared for the flight. Once the announcement was made, he became giddy with excitement, ready to start his next adventure: working in the oilfield, on the North Slope! He knew, without a doubt, that it was going to be exciting to lay eyes on a place that few have been able to see and experience. And most importantly, he was going to earn money being there.

His seat was 1C. First row on the aisle, easy access to the restroom but, more importantly, easy access to the exit. If there was an emergency, he would be one of the first to escape and survive.

As he sat in his seat, he watched the others board the plane. He was perplexed that there wasn't a more formal boarding process. The doors opened, and people quickly stowed their belongings and sat in their assigned seats. The whole process lasted about fifteen minutes from the time the door opened, and everyone stowed their carry-ons until the boarding door closed. Many walking by him were quick to take note of his blue helmet. He was sure they were jealous!

The flight attendants did their final pre-flight checks, making sure that items were properly stowed, seat backs and tray tables were in the up position, and all occupants were properly belted in.

"Good morning, this is Jeffrey, your captain. I'm accompanied in the cockpit by Stuart and three of the best flight attendants: Cherie, Mabel and Bertha. Sit back and enjoy today's flight. We'll push back from the gate momentarily, de-ice and be on our way. We're expecting a smooth flight and a flight time of one hour and forty minutes."

As the plane pushed away from the gate, the flight attendants began their passenger pre-flight safety briefing. He tuned it out and put on his headphones. "I'm no rookie to flying. They're all the same. Blah, blah, blah." Bob's thoughts turned to the awesome opportunity he was getting ready to experience, working on the North Slope, in the oilfield. Time slowed to a crawl while waiting for the de-icing equipment to arrive. The seconds ticked slowly away into minutes, into what seemed like an eternity. Finally, this fancy truck arrived with an articulating arm with some kind of nozzle attached. It sprayed the entire plane with a kind of pink liquid, which he assumed was like windshield wiper fluid.

Finally, the first turbofan fired off, spinning up to speed, followed by the second turbofan engaging and whirring up to speed. The pilots cycled the engines, released the brake, and slowly taxied toward the runway. Still lost in deep thought, Bob was surprised when the guy sitting next to him nudged him and said, “Hey bub, where y’all headed?”

Bob, a bit agitated because of the interruption, was curt in his response, “The oilfield.”

Kurt, his nosy neighbor, thought, “No shit. That’s where we’re all going. Obviously, that little blue helmet is too tight on his melon.”

One hour into the flight, the staticky intercom chimed, and the pilot announced, “We had a great tail wind and have made great time. We’ll begin our descent in about ten minutes.”

Bob’s excitement went to the next level. “I’m about to become an oilfield worker!” he thought. He could hardly sit still in his seat for the approach and landing. Once they broke through the cloud layer, it was nothing but gray sky, white-covered nothingness, and lights illuminating different facilities. As quickly as they broke through the cloudy barrier, they were impacting the ground. The pilot seemed to be heavy on the brakes as Bob was jerked forward and with the abrupt stop.

The plane came to a stop and then made a turn right on the runway, which didn’t appear wide enough to turn around on. They taxied slowly to the runway apron, where three large white motorcoaches awaited the arriving passengers. Bob thought, "Rock star buses – how cool is that!" He was the first one up and out of his seat when the chime dinged, notifying passengers it was safe to stand and gather their belongings. With his helmet securely strapped to his head, he threw on his backpack and was the first in line waiting for the door to open.

When the door was opened, a blast of cold air caught him off guard. It must be 100 degrees below zero out there. The reality is that it was cold, a frigid -20°F, with wind gusts of 25 mph. He walked down the stairs onto the snow-covered, frozen tarmac. The security officer at the bottom of the stairs directed him toward the waiting buses.

"I'm not really sure which bus to get on, but I know that I'm going to some place called Alpine." Bob perused the reader board on the front of the buses; they all had weird acronyms, and then he saw it, a small, older school bus parked on the other side of the motorcoaches. Across the front it read "Alpine." He made a beeline for the bus, almost running to get out of the cold and wind.

The driver sat atop the steps, waiting for passengers to board. As they boarded, he asked, "Name?"

Bob made his way to the back of the bus, as all the signs indicated to start seating from the back. He was annoyed when other passengers didn't follow the directions. "They must be special," he thought.

The passengers were all off the plane, and each bus driver stood and gave a safety briefing. "Welcome back to work. The current temperature is -20°F. We are in normal operating conditions, but there is a front moving through tomorrow and we may go into phase conditions. Be sure to take your arctic gear with you as you travel to your work location. Traction devices are required at all work locations. Have a safe, productive hitch."

The Alpine bus was the last to leave the tarmac and drove toward what appeared to be the camp. The bus parked in the middle of the area. The driver informed the passengers that they were awaiting the arrival of the "Otter" from Alpine. Fifteen minutes passed, then thirty, and finally, after an hour, the bus driver made an announcement: "The Otter had a mechanical issue and won't be flying today. We will be driving to Alpine." There was some grumbling amongst the passengers but not Bob. What he didn't realize was that the ride is about two hours, and the heaters barely work on the bus.

His backpack still in hand and his blue helmet still affixed to his head, he sat back, relaxed, and dozed in and out of sleep on the bumpy ride. There wasn't much to see along the ride: everything was covered in snow, the ground was pretty flat, and every once in a while, they would see the lights of some kind of facility or drilling rig. The scenery never changed. It was nothing like he had imagined. He expected mountains and wildlife galore.

Two hours and fifteen minutes later, they drove into a large facility, smaller than the other ones, but still bigger than anything he had experienced in his life. The bus rolled to a stop outside a pair of doors, the entrance to the camp. The driver asked, "Anyone new here?" Bob reluctantly raised his hand and appeared to be the only newbie. "Sir, you'll have to attend the safety briefing and orientation at security. It's up the stairs and to the right." The other passengers, once released, were quick to get off the bus and head into the building. Bob double-checked his blue helmet and secured his backpack to his back.

When he stepped off the bus into the cold, it didn't appear to be as frigid as it was at that other place, and there was no wind. The woman in front of him held the door open until he was close enough to grab it himself. He followed the line into the building and, looking for the Security Office, to the right. He was greeted by an older gentleman in a blue uniform, complete with an embroidered badge and a name tag. "Welcome to Alpine. I'm Bob. I'll be giving you the safety briefing and orientation, and then we'll call your foreman and have him come meet you."

"I'm Bob too!"

Security Bob guided him down the hallway to a conference room, where a TV screen and DVD player were set up. Bob was handed an information packet to read; it had a map of the facility, where to muster if there was an alarm, the hours for the chow hall, and pages of information about the facility. "When you're ready, push play, and the video will start. I'll come back in about forty-five minutes." As Security Bob left the room, he chuckled to himself because Bob had yet to remove his blue helmet.

Bob hit the play button after perusing the information packet. He watched with great intent. There was some pretty cool stuff in the video. It talked about wildlife around the facilities – polar bears, caribou, and arctic and red foxes. It talked about driving and the buddy system, the extreme dangers of exposure to the cold, and, most importantly, about personal safety. Security Bob arrived just as the video was finishing up and asked, "Any questions?"

"No sir. When do I go to work?"

"Who do you work for, and do you know who your foreman is?"

"I work for Alaska Petrol Constructors, my foreman is Steve, and here's his number." Several attempts were made to call the number, first couple of times it just rang and rang, then it went to voicemail the next several attempts.

Finally, someone picked up, "This is Steve."

"Hi Steve. This is Bob with security. I have Bob here, and he's ready to go to work."

"I'm sorry. I'm in a meeting for the next hour. Can you take him to the chow hall and get him something to drink and a snack?"

Security Bob hung up and informed Bob of the conversation. "If you'd like, I'll show you where your room is, you can drop off your stuff, and then I'll show you the chow hall."

"My stuff stays with me. I'm not comfortable leaving it anywhere. I will take a cup of coffee though." They left the conference room and walked down the hallway to a flight of stairs, which took them down another hall and past the chow hall. They walked past the dish room, which looked like something you'd find in a restaurant or school cafeteria.

Around the corner were rows of glass-door refrigerators and freezers, like you'd see in a convenience store. They were packed with all kinds of pre-packaged foods and drinks. There was a soda fountain and an industrial sized row of coffee pots, a full sized salad bar, and the most beautiful case of fresh-made donuts and pastries. Bob settled on an apple fritter and a cup of coffee.

Security Bob left him seated at one of the tables in the chow hall to enjoy his snack. While he was sitting there, several people wandered through into the food area, each coming out with some kind of snack and a beverage. It was hard not to notice Bob sitting there; the blue helmet was like a neon sign on his head. Bob waited patiently for the arrival of Steve, his foreman and new boss.

Steve arrived around 5:15 p.m., which was close to the end of the workday. It wasn't hard to figure out who Bob was when Steve walked into the chow hall. He had already been informed to look for the guy wearing the blue bicycle helmet. Steve thought it was a joke and that people were just messing with him, but that wasn't the case. Steve walked directly to Bob and introduced himself. "Howdy, I'm Steve. Welcome to Alpine. Since it's the end of the day, you get a pass on doing any work today. The workday starts at 6:00 a.m. tomorrow. I'll show ya to your room if you want."

Bob was disappointed that he was going to have to wait until tomorrow to start doing work, but there wasn't anything he could do about it. "I'm just gonna hang out here, eat dinner, and then go to my room, and I'll see you in the morning. Where should I meet you?" He was instructed to meet in the job trailer, out on the work location. Steve showed him on the map exactly where he needed to be. Bob thanked him, and Steve left.

Bob noticed there was a line going into the kitchen area. "That must be the chow line." He strapped his backpack back on and got in line. Most of the folks were laughing, joking, and cutting up. They seemed to be a fairly good bunch of folks. What Bob didn't realize was some of the joking was about the guy in the blue bicycle helmet – him. Bob was surprised by the amount of the food on the line. It was like a buffet, and they were grilling steaks to order. It was like going to one of those buffets in Las Vegas.

He filled himself on steak, baked potato, grilled asparagus, a salad, and for dessert a piece of apple pie with soft serve ice cream. This is going to be a great place to work he thought to himself. A fully belly and a long day traveling brought on the after-dinner slowdown, so he decided to go find his assigned room. It wasn't too hard to figure out thanks to his ability to read the map. Settling in for the night, he brushed his teeth, donned his pajamas, and removed his blue helmet. He was far too excited to sleep though. So far, this adventure was shaping up to be a great one. He laid in bed for what seemed like hours, fading in and out of sleep. Finally, at about 3a.m. he decided, "I have had enough of trying to sleep. I saw there is a gym here. I'm going to find it and work out!" He brushed his teeth, dressed in sweats, and carefully strapped on his blue helmet.

He entered the gym and was impressed how much equipment there was. It was like most commercial gyms. There were several other people working out, and he wondered if they couldn't sleep either. He found an empty treadmill and programmed it for a workout. He started at a slow walk, transitioned into a speed walk, and then shifted to a jogging speed. Forty-five minutes later, he was drenched in sweat and began his cooldown. Once the treadmill came to a complete stop, he stepped off and found an area to stretch.

The workout was now complete, and it was time to go shower, eat breakfast, and prepare to start his new life as an oilfield worker. His excitement was overwhelming. He returned to his room where he carefully removed his sweats and his blue helmet. With great pride and care, he cleaned and dried his helmet. The shower was warm and had one of those massage jet shower heads. It felt great! He showered, shaved, brushed his teeth, donned his work clothes, and last, but not least, put on his blue helmet. Just prior to leaving the room, he strapped his backpack, with all his worldly possessions, on his back.

He made his way to the chow hall. There was a long line of guys and gals all dressed in similar blue fire-retardant clothing. The air was filled with the smell of fresh cooked bacon, and he knew immediately what he was having for breakfast. The food line didn't disappoint. There was fresh fruit, oatmeal, scrambled eggs, bacon, sausage, hash-browns, and pancakes, and the chef was making omelets to order. In addition, there were boxes of cereal, yogurt, bananas, apples, raisins, and just about anything you could want. Sitting in the chow hall, he ate his breakfast and watched others. They were watching him too – it was hard not to pay attention to the blue helmet attached to his head.

Steve walked up to where he was seated, "Mornin'. If you're done with breakfast, I'll walk with you out to the job trailer for the toolbox meeting."

"Thanks. Let me take my dishes to the dish room."

Steve waited patiently as Bob scraped his plates and placed them in the racks for washing. Steve and Bob donned their coats and traction devices for the walk across the frozen gravel pad. When they stepped out the door, it was quickly evident that the temperature had fallen over night. Steve said, "It's gonna be a cold sumbitch today. It's -45°F right now. I hope you brought lots of warm gear. I'll make sure you have PPE – hard hat, safety glasses, and gloves."

Bob responded, "I brought my own, I'm good."

They entered the job trailer, and there were about ten guys sitting around, drinking coffee, talking about their last R&R. They all looked at Bob. Steve introduced him and said, "We have a new teammate. This is Bob. Y'all need to watch out for him."

Several nodded their heads towards Bob, some gave a, "hey," and others were silent. Steve lined out the work for the day, and, as a team, they identified hazards and how to mitigate them. Steve paired Bob up with Gary for the day. At the conclusion of the meeting, they dressed in their cold weather gear and headed out into the facility to start work.

Steve attended a couple of meetings, caught-up on paperwork and decided to go check on his crew, especially the new guy. Two hours into the workday, Steve located Bob working on the second story of a scaffold platform. Steve signaled Bob to come down from the platform. Bob struggled a little bit since he was still wearing his backpack. When he was safely on the ground, Steve said, "We need to get you a proper hard hat and stow your backpack."

Bob rebutted with, "There is nothing wrong with my helmet, and my backpack has everything I own, and it stays with me!"

Steve said, "I'm pretty sure that blue bicycle helmet isn't ANSI-rated, and I don't need you getting hurt."

Bob stated, "This helmet will protect. Besides there isn't anything falling out of the sky."

Steve started to get irritated and frustrated. "If you don't wear the right gear, I can't let you work."

Bob grunted, "Whatever."

At this point, Steve had to walk away before he let his anger fly.

Bob decided, "Maybe this isn't the place for me." Two hours later, Bob didn't show up for lunch in the chow hall. Steve questioned his crew as to Bob's whereabouts. No one seemed to know. They hadn't seen him in quite a while. Steve went to the Security Office and notified the on-duty captain one of his guys was missing. An immediate field-wide announcement was made that a man was missing. Description was given, including "last seen wearing a blue bicycle helmet."

Two hours into a field-wide manhunt, a radio communication came through security. Bob had been located. He was found hitch-hiking on the ice road between fields. He was picked-up by a truck driver bringing drill pipe to Alpine. He was delivered to the

Security Office. Arrangements were made to transport Bob off the slope, back to Anchorage.

Luckily, Bob was found. He could have become lost and died from exposure. The ice road between fields is about thirty miles, and it is about 800 miles to Anchorage. I guess if you are more worried about your blue bicycle helmet, distance doesn't matter.

CHAPTER TWO

THE ANUS IS ON YOU & THE WILD JUICE CHASE

The first new major facility in over a decade was in the throes of construction. There were approximately 1,000 craftmen working in the field and a management team of about forty. Construction was not going as smoothly as it should have; design and fabrication issues were slowing the construction progress. There was a huge amount of pressure to get the new facility and field online. Production was anticipated to be upwards of 60-80,000 barrels per day.

One of the measures put into place to try to understand the issues and provide resolution was for the management team to meet daily. Sometimes the meeting lasted several hours, and on this particular day, there were a number of new issues brought to the table.

"So, tell me, Ron, what's on your mind? What's keeping us from achieving completion?" asked Dan, the Company manager.

Ron, the contractor manager, thought long and hard before he responded. Everyone in the room was interested and staring at Ron. Some even sat at the edge of their seats, anticipating what the excuse was today for not making the planned progress. After a minute, Ron inched forward, placed his elbows on the table, and interlaced his fingers. "Well, Dan, there are several things keeping us from being successful. Every day, there seems to be more incomplete work identified coming out of the fabrication yards. It's hard to manage the scope when it continually changes."

Dan looked at Ron and stated, "We knew there was going to be work that was incomplete from the fabrication yards. You should have built that into your plan."

"We did, based on the information you provided about what was incomplete. Your incomplete work lists seem to be incomplete. It's hard to estimate and plan for constant change to the scope." Ron was becoming a little agitated by the nonchalant, cavalier attitude of Dan.

"What else?" Dan asked condescendingly.

"Materials. We have no responsibility for buying the materials to complete the work. Every day, all day, we continue to identify materials that you provided, that are incorrect, or that are still not here. It's hard to do work without the right materials." Ron knew this would only irritate Dan, but he had to be honest and upfront.

"So, you want me to have materials magically appear? You know that it takes time to get them here. We're in the middle of nowhere!"

Another issue was having the right craft to perform the work. At a time when the construction industry was booming, it was difficult, at best, to hire qualified, competent people. This issue was brought forth at the meeting, and a pretty heated discussion ensued between Dan and Ron. At the end of the discussion, Dan looked his counterpart square in the eye and said, "Well, Ron, the anus is on you!"

The guy next to me leaned over and whispered, "Did he just say the 'anus' is on you?"

I whispered back, "I think he means 'onus.'" There were several perplexed looks around the room. The meeting was adjourned, and folks went back to their offices.

The following morning, around 4:30 a.m., I was getting a cup of coffee when the Ron approached me.

"I need your help."

"Sure, what do you need?"

Ron stretched and said, "I didn't get any sleep last night."

I asked, "Do you have a snoring roommate? Bad pillows? Lumpy mattress?"

Ron chuckled and said, "No. I was so worried after yesterday's meeting that I was up all night looking for the anus on me." We both had a good laugh and headed off to start work for the day.

Fast forward three days…

Dan began, "Good afternoon. Thanks for being here. Together we're going to make the work happen, and the Company will start to make money. Ron, how are things going?"

Ron, being in his normal jovial mood with a dry sense of humor, said "Well, Dan, I wish I could say that this was as fun as duck hunting, but we're continuing to not find the ducks."

"What do you mean? I'm not a duck hunter," Dan replied in his all-too-typical, condescending manner.

Ron, continued, jokingly, "My guys are ready for the kill but are struggling to find the right materials. They are told materials are here and that they have been received and receipted, but no one seems to be able to lay their hands on the materials they need to do the work. For instance, all the insulation materials we need, which would be truckloads, just don't appear to be here."

Dan's face reddened. Everyone knew that he was fixing to lose his cool and have, yet another meltdown. "I don't care what it takes, what the excuse is. These guys need to be productive and completing work every day! It sounds like just another excuse as to why work is not getting done. This is BS!"

Ron replied, keeping his cool, "It's not an excuse. It's reality. We are scouring the warehouse, scouring the yard. We brought in more people to expedite materials. We just can't find the materials we need when we need them."

"This is ridiculous! You're telling me we have people out there on a wild juice chase, looking for materials!?" The room was silent, perplexed that we were chasing "wild juice." The meeting continued for another hour before being adjourned.

That evening, in the chow line, as I filled my water glass at the soda fountain, Ron approached me. "I hope you're not drinking some of that wild juice, but if you are, let me know if it tastes any different than normal juice..."

CHAPTER THREE

FLUFFY TAILED POLAR BEARS

There is an abundance of wildlife located on the North Slope of Alaska. Often, it wanders through the facilities where oil drilling and production occurs. Caribou, foxes (red and arctic), bears (black, brown, and polar), migratory birds, and muskox are commonly observed. Oilfield workers are given training on how to avoid interaction with and impact on wildlife. This story relates to polar bear awareness training and the actions taken to keep the bear and the workers safe.

A lot of new construction occurs during the winter months, allowing the oil companies to build ice roads for access, rather than normal gravel roads. Many of the pipelines that crisscross the tundra are built only in the winter because of the access needed to perform construction. The typical winter construction season lasts from December to May and varies from year to year depending on temperature and the scope of work to be completed. Unlike drilling operations, which are twenty-four hours per day, construction is usually a single day shift, twelve hours. The reality is that during the winter, there is little difference in "daylight."

The construction of a new series of pipelines required working around the clock. This was the only practical way to ensure that work would be completed in the short construction season. The team was divided into day and night shift work. The night shift, although a smaller crew, was critical to being able to complete work during the day.

On this particular night, the crew of about twenty-four was working on installing the piling foundations for a pipe bridge. The temperatures were subzero, and the visibility was limited due to blowing snow. Other than the foreman for the crew, the only other oversight was an HSE specialist (health, safety, and environment). The HSE specialist's primary function was to ensure crews were working safely. The crew was about halfway through their shift when someone noticed movement off in the distance. Because of the potential of a polar bear being in the area, someone had to become the "Bear Watch." The crew was already shorthanded, so they asked the HSE specialist to take on the duties. He gladly accepted. Being from Lousiana, he thought it cool that he might get to see a real live bear.

About thirty minutes later, the radio chirped, "Attention all hands: a bear has been observed. Stop all work and meet at the job trailer. This is not a drill." The crew quickly powered everything down and evacuated to the job trailer. An emergency call was placed to security. By the book, procedures were followed, and everyone was safe. Security gathered their gear, including a shotgun and shells, to investigate. Even though lethal rounds are often carried, they are rarely used. They are for an absolute, imminent threat. Most of the time, cracker rounds (for noise) are used to scare the bear or other wildlife away.

Sometimes there are non-lethal rounds like bean bags or rubber bullets.

Security arrived on scene as quickly as possible to investigate. After searching for forty-five minutes, they did find tracks in the snow, which eventually lead them to an arctic fox den. Although some might ask how you could confuse a bear and a fox, with poor lighting and visibility, it is possible.

The HSE specialist was thanked for acting quickly, making sure the crew was safe and proper procedures followed. He did take some razzing from several folks for not being able to tell the difference between a bear and a fox, and affectionately became known as Billy Bear.

The story doesn't end there though…

Fast-forward three days in time. Billy Bear again was assigned the duties of Bear Watch. He was certain that he would not overreact again and was comfortable with his duties. But halfway through the shift, he noticed a silhouette on the horizon. It was too far off to tell exactly what it was, so out of concern that it might be a real polar bear this time, he made the announcement over the radio, "Attention all hands, a bear has been observed. Stop all work and meet at the job trailer. This is not a drill." Once the crew was safe in the job trailer, he notified Security.

The security team quickly assembled and headed out into the night to investigate. Tracks were observed in the snow, fairly small for a polar bear. Again, they lead to an arctic fox den. The all clear was given to return to work.

The following day, word quickly spread through camp that Billy Bear had called in another false alarm on a polar bear. Was he the little boy that cried wolf? Surely not.

To help, someone, who will remain anonymous, assembled a wildlife identification poster. The poster had pictures of every bear imaginable: black bear, brown bear, cinnamon bear, polar bear, Winnie-the-Pooh bear, Yogi Bear. The poster also had pictures of every imaginable fox: red fox, blue fox, arctic fox, and Redd Fox the comedian.

The big takeaways for most involved in this story: perform better training on wildlife identification and do not put a guy from the Deep South in charge of Bear Watch.

CHAPTER FOUR

I'LL SEE YOU AT CHRISTMAS

Workers in the oilfield often work a rotation schedule, meaning that they work for a period, then have a period off. The R&R, as it is affectionately known, is the off period, typically equal to the amount of time spent working, and means "rest and relaxation." It is time to enjoy the fruits of your bounty and spend time with your friends and family, doing the things you love. Schedules vary quite a bit, everything from one week on/one week off to six weeks on/two weeks off.

This is the story of one individual, prior to the Oil Companies limiting time at work...

The 1965 metallic blue, with a white top, four-door Rambler pulled up to the gate of the parking lot at the Tampa Bay Airport. It was still in pristine condition. Whoever owned it took exceptionally good care of it. Even though it was beyond being a classic car, it did not show it's thirty-two years of age and had less than a hundred thousand miles on it. It was hard to believe that it was all original and wasn't a restoration.

The parking lot attendant leaned out of the booth. “Good morning, Mr. G. It must be time to fly back to Alaska for work. I don’t know why you park that beautiful car here. It is a classic. You should buy a new car, since the only places you drive it are here and to the grocery store.”

Mr. G smiled and turned a little red with embarrassment. “I love this car. I bought it brand new. It is my baby, and I feel safe parking it here while I’m at work. Especially since my mom should not be driving it. I know that it costs me a few dollars to park it here while I disappear for work, but I know it’s in your capable hands.”

Blushing, the attendant smiled, “You know, I have nothing to do with your car, other than being here to give you a parking ticket so that when you return, you can pay your bill. You know, you could always leave me the keys, and I would take care of your baby.”

“That would be fine, but I am the only one that has ever driven this beauty. Not even my own mother has laid hands on the steering wheel.” Mr. G lovingly gripped the color matched blue steering wheel, caressing it like his favorite gal.

“Are you going to be home for St. Patty’s Day this year? Ya know, it is only a couple of weeks away. Even though I’m not Irish, I love me some corned beef and cabbage.”

Mr. G’s smile disappeared, “I’m not Irish. I’m German. I do not celebrate a day where the goal is to get inebriated. I will be home for Christmas, as usual.”

Mr. G’s story is interesting. Now in his late sixties and never married, his primary goal was to make money to take care of his now aging mother. He worked as a construction engineer on the Trans-Alaska Pipeline (TAPS). His home away from home was Pump Station 3, located approximately one hundred miles south of

Prudhoe Bay, Alaska. He would leave for the work, typically, in early March and return in December to celebrate the holidays with his mother.

CHAPTER FIVE

THE MAD CRAPPER

Tony was sitting in his office, debating whether to call me at Pump Station 4 of the Trans-Alaska Pipeline. The current time was 8:30 a.m. He decided, "why not?"

The phone rang, once, twice, three times, and on the fourth ring it went to the answering machine. Even though I was sitting at my desk, I was in the middle of sending a note on the computer using the PROFS system, which is DOS-based and antiquated, and if you do not enter information properly, the message does not send or makes little sense. You must remember to add an asterisk at the start of every line.

The crackling speaker of the $99 answering machine came to life. "Hey Bud, it's me Tony. I was just giving you a ring to see if you heard what happened at Annex 1 last night." Annex 1 is one of the many camps located on the North Slope of Alaska. It is a few miles from Pump Station 1. The camp is filled with oilfield workers who are contracted through a third-party company to provide a variety of services to the owner-operators of the facilities.

The camp is run down and in dire need of updating,

but it is a warm place to stay, and the food is pretty decent. There is a gym, pool tables, ping pong tables, table-top shuffleboard, and cribbage. Additionally, there are usually puzzles in various stages of completion on tabletops in the recreation area.

I finished my report in PROFS and decided to give Tony a call back. I was curious as to the events that occurred in the camp. I dialed and patiently waited for the phone to start ringing. There was an odd delay usually, maybe due to the cold weather affecting the land lines, then, "Hey, Tony, what's the word, dude?"

There was a brief pause, followed by a chuckle. "You're not gonna believe what happened at the camp. Some guy trashed his room at Annex 1. He busted up the desk, broke the window, cut-up the bed, and then defecated on the floor."

I started laughing. "You know April Fool's Day is still a few months away, right?"

"Serious as a heart attack. That shit's true!" Tony said.

I started laughing. "Yeah, and I'm the pope."

Tony, feeling a little dismayed that I didn't believe him, said, "Well, it's true, but I gotta run to a meeting." The phone line went dead.

Tony was always up to practical jokes; he didn't take the job or life too seriously. It made the job easier to do. I returned to my workload and started working on my next assignment, a review of drawings for an upcoming project. The stack of engineering drawings seemed to be a foot thick, and most of the drawings were for reference, rather than for the actual work.

The phone ringing again was a welcome interruption after staring at drawings for the last two hours. Additionally, my highlighter was running out of fluid, and I was going to have to take a break to find a replacement in the less-than-adequately-stocked supply cabinet.

"Hey, it's Tony again. I just got an update. All that stuff I told you is true. And here is the best part. It was YOUR room."

I chuckled. "You are a funny guy, but there's no way. I think you are just messing with me."

"Dude, I'm totally serious. It was your room."

I really didn't think about it much after I hung up the phone. I had a new challenge to overcome, finding a replacement for the highlighter which was quickly running dry. Down the hall I wandered, to the supply cabinet. I was digging through the metal cabinet, partially filled with office supplies and personal protective gear, when Doug, my boss, walked through the door of the office.

"Hey Doug, how's it going?"

Doug seemed to be deep in thought. "It's going. Do you have a minute to chat?"

"Of course, I always have time for the boss. What's up?"

Doug stuttered, stammered, and then replied, "I don't know how to ask, or what to say, but are you pissed off about something?"

I half laughed. "What do I have to be pissed off about? I have a good job, work with a good team, make decent money, and have plenty of work to keep me busy."

"Well, I don't know if you have heard any of the rumors this morning, but one of the rooms at Annex 1 was trashed last night."

I nodded and replied, "Yup, I've heard the rumors. Pretty funny story, but what does it have to do with me?"

The look on Doug's face got very serious. "The room that was trashed was your room at Annex 1. I have to ask if it was you that did all those things."

I was perplexed by Doug's question. How could

anyone think that I would be capable of those things? "Well, for starters, if I was pissed off about something, I would be man enough to say something. Secondly, I'm not the kind of person that would take out my anger, frustrations, or emotions that way. I am baffled that anyone could think that I was capable of such behavior. It's not me!"

Doug, in typical managerial fashion, washed the emotion from his face. "I had to ask. I don't know you very well, so I had to ask. I will let you know as things move forward. I didn't think you were that kind of person, but it's really hard to read people sometimes. The investigation is still ongoing, and I will let you know if anything else comes up."

After the conversation ended and Doug left my office, I needed a break. I grabbed my gear bag, hardhat, safety glasses, coat, and gloves and headed out to my pickup truck. The drive to the job site is about an hour, up Atigun Pass to the Chandalar Shelf. I sat in the truck while the diesel engine warmed up to operating temperature. I thought about the conversation that had occurred in my office. The idea that someone could think I was capable of such behavior caused me discontent.

The drive from Pump Station 4, down the valley to the bottom of the pass, was beautiful. The sun shone brightly on the snow-covered peaks. The caribou, several hundred of them, meandered aimlessly across the frozen tundra. It was like living in a post card picture.

I arrived on the job site and checked-in with the foreman before going to visit the crews doing work.

Jack asked, "How was the drive down? It was pretty windy and snowy this morning."

I could tell by Jack's demeanor that something else was on his mind. "The drive was good. No snow, clear and beautiful. The caribou were in the normal spot. Nothing out of the ordinary. What else is going on?" I asked.

Jack hemmed and hawed, and finally asked, "Is the rumor true?"

I knew exactly what he was talking about but played dumb. "What rumor is that?"

Reluctantly, Jack responded, "You know, the rumor that you took a shit in one of the rooms at Annex 1."

I momentarily just stared at him and then started laughing. "If you must know, yep, I did it. I had to go and knew there was no way I would be able to squeeze my cheeks together long enough to make it down the hallway to the restroom. Besides, that's what housekeeping is for, to clean up after us." Jack's eyes widened with my response. I started laughing. "It wasn't me, if it's true. I'm surprised how quickly the rumor has spread! I would guess that the rumors flow faster than the oil in that pipeline over there."

I left the office trailer and walked the job, talking to most of the crew of about thirty people. Even though many looked at me as "the boss," I always considered myself just another one of the guys, and the guy who took the blame for anything that went wrong. I think most everyone on the job enjoyed working with me because of my easy-going demeanor and ability to give and take "smack."

I looked at my watch and realized that it was now after lunch, and I didn't bring anything with me. If I left now, I would be able to make it back to Pump Station 4 for afternoon break. It was a short walk back to where my truck was parked, and, thankfully, I had left it running. It was plenty warm as I took off my jacket, gloves, and hardhat.

I pulled out of the site onto the highway. Even though it is officially part of the Alaska highway system and maintained by state road crews, it is nothing more than a two-lane gravel highway, laid across the tundra to support the construction of the Trans-Alaska Pipeline and supply the industry with all the goods required to produce oil. The road eventually transitions into blacktop pavement a couple hundred miles to the south, somewhere just north of Fairbanks.

The drive was beautiful, the weather was still clear, and it was hard not to get lost in the scenery. The road going north up Atigun Pass seems to be a lot less steep than the north side of the pass, but it is a much slower climb. At the top, there was a pullout area, so I decided to stop and just look down the awesome valley to the north. The serenity and peace of the snow-capped mountains made me feel like I was one with nature, one with God. I thanked him for the beautiful scenery, the blessed life.

I remembered that I have one of the cameras issued for taking job-site photos, a Sony Mavica. Cell phones were not equipped with cameras back then, and digital technology was in its infancy. I powered on the camera and waited for it to read the 3.5" floppy disk. The camera was ready. I snapped the first photo, waited for it to save on the floppy, snapped another, tried the zoom function, and snapped several others. It was a slow process, but I managed to take about a dozen photos before rolling up the window to resume my drive.

I depressed the brake, shifted into drive, and slowly began to re-enter the roadway. About the time I was up to the speed limit, an eighteen wheeler came roaring around the corner, black smoke pouring from its twin stacks, struggling to make it up the grade with its load. I thought about the guy behind the wheel and wondered why anyone would want to drive this road for a living.

I sped up to put some distance between me and that eighty thousand pounds of bone crushing mass. I knew that if he were right behind me going down the pass, I would stand little chance if he couldn't slow down or lost control.

There was no sign of the truck as I wound around the winding road, and I could see the bottom of the pass where it turned into a straight road again. Once the road straightened, it wasn't flat, but a gradual decline until you were down on the valley floor. As I put more distance between me and the truck, I finally saw his headlights rounding one of the corners about midway down the pass. He must have geared all the way down, to not lose control coming down the pass.

Danger had been averted, and my thoughts returned to the story of the destruction at Annex 1. I started laughing out loud at the preposterous thought of others thinking that I had done all those things, especially the part about defecating in the room. I had heard stories from days gone by about guys who would defecate to make a point, whether it was poor living conditions, a bad boss, low pay, or bad food.

I arrived at the security gate at Pump Station 4, and the guard opened the window and asked for my badge. "Hey, John. Where ya been? Out fishing?"

Ralph was always trying to be funny, if he only knew that we referred to him as Barney Fife. "I had to get out of the office, so I went down to Chandalar to check on my guys. Anything exciting happening today?"

Ralph just shook his head side to side. "We ain't had no excitement since that feller had a heart attack two months ago. Pretty boring around here, but I like it that way!" After logging me in, he handed back my badge and gave me the nod to go. The rolling gate came to life and slowly rolled out of the way.

I put my truck in drive and accelerated to the speed

limit, 5 mph. I drove past the guard shack and waved at Ralph. I drove past the construction camp, which consisted of ATCO trailers (ATCO is a company that manufacturers portable buildings) and the P.L.Q. (permanent living quarters), turned left at the tank farm, drove past the turbine building, turned left at the end of the road, and then turned left again onto the road on the other side of the control room, where the construction office was located. I parked outside the office, shut off the truck, and gathered my paperwork and gear.

I entered the office, a double wide trailer subdivided into offices separated by partitions into cubicles. I walked to my cubicle, dropped my stuff on the desk, and headed out the back door to the porta potty.

After re-entering the office, I visited the table which held a two-burner Bunn-O-Matic coffee maker, a tray of donuts and pastries, and a tray of vegetables. I grabbed an apple fritter and a cup of hot, overcooked coffee and went to my desk.

I depressed the button on the camera to eject the floppy disk. Of course, it never worked on the first try. Two more pushes of the button, and the disk finally ejected. I put it into the desktop computer located on my desk and started the file transfer process. I wanted to see how well my pictures turned out.

The computer was slowly copying the contents of the disk onto the computer hard drive when Doug walked through the back door of the office. He walked directly to my cubicle, ignoring the other occupants – the safety guy, one of the other field engineers, and the superintendent.

"Have you got a minute to talk? I have more info regarding the events at Annex 1."

I was really interested to hear what the latest and greatest rumor was, so I was quick to say, "Sure."

Doug said, "Maybe we should go to my office. It's a little more private." I grabbed my jacket and followed Doug out the door to his office, which was in the facility operations building across the parking lot.

We entered Doug's office, and he closed the door. I sat in the chair in front of his desk, thinking about the fresh apple fritter and now cooling cup of coffee on my desk. I should have at least brought the coffee with me.

"So, here's the latest and greatest information. Apparently, the damage to the room at Annex 1 is true, and it has happened at Pump Stations 2 and 3, as well," Doug stated.

I half laughed. "Well, that definitely rules out the potential that I'm the guy. I have done projects at Pump Station 2 and 3, but I've never stayed in either of the camps."

The look on Doug's face was that of dismay. It was hard to tell if he was looking forward to terminating my employment or if he was perplexed because I was no longer a suspect. "The investigation is still ongoing, but that was the latest information that I received from security. You can go back to your office. I will let you know more once I know more. Thanks."

I stood, donned my jacket, shook Doug's hand, and said, "Thanks. I'll be in my office." The short walk back to my office was filled with thoughts of the day coming to an end and wondering if the real story would eventually come out. I sat at my desk, looking at the cold cup of coffee, and the now air-dried apple fritter. I tossed the apple fritter in the trash and logged into PROFS to check messages.

The good news: no new messages. I thought to myself, "Maybe I should just stick a fork in today. I have had enough." I logged out of PROFS and off the computer. I put on my jacket, grabbed my backpack, and headed out the back door. It was a short walk to my room in the construction camp, the sun was starting to disappear, and the wind was picking up. The temperature had definitely fallen, so my pace quickened to get to camp and out of the cold.

Once in the camp, I removed my work boots and changed into slippers for walking around the camp. There was a "boot room" just inside the door, and the intent was to keep personnel from tracking snow and ice into the camp, or mud in the summer. It felt good to get out of the boots. Although they were comfortable, I hated wearing them all day.

I wandered down the hallway to my room, hoping that my roommates were not there. Thankfully, I had the room to myself for a couple of minutes. I dug through my bag and found sweats and tennis shoes. I hated living out of a duffle bag, but I was constantly on the road for different projects in half a dozen different locations.

I figured I would catch a quick workout before dinner. I donned my jacket and boots once again and made the walk to the PLQ. I had the gym to myself, which meant I could put on some good music and not worry about having to listen to someone else's choice in music. The gym was nothing special. It consisted of a Universal Gym, a treadmill, and an exercise bike. There were also a few free weights and dumbbells. I hit all ten stations on the Universal for a couple of rounds and followed it with thirty minutes on the exercise bike.

I managed to work up a good sweat, burn off the thought of eating that apple fritter, and relieve some stress. The dinner chow line would be opening in about ten minutes, so I headed to the TV room to catch a few minutes of the news. Several others had the same idea. It was not uncommon to find people hanging out in the TV room prior to the chow line opening.

The room slowly cleared, and I was the last one to leave. I didn't like being the first one in the chow line, even though I was starving. Tonight's meal would be like any other. Mediocre food, warm, and it filled the void. I grabbed a tray, utensils, salad bowl, and a plate. I waited patiently while the guy in front of me made a ginormous salad. I don't think he missed anything on the salad bar. I made my normal salad: lettuce, spinach, carrots, radishes, almonds, and ranch dressing. As I approached the entrées, I remembered it was steak night. Bonus!

The head chef asked, "Steak?"

I replied, "Yes, well and blackened, please."

It only took a few seconds, and as he handed me the plate with a steak on it, he commented, "Now don't be leavin' that steak in your room like you done at Annex 1. Crapper."

I just shook my head and laughed. "Maybe I should take some gravy and make you a special surprise. You know it wasn't me that did that."

I laughed to myself at how quickly the rumor had spread. We were 150 miles from Annex 1, but the rumor was already here at Pump Station 4. I wandered into the dining area and found an empty seat with a couple of the crew from one of the jobs.

I sat down and Gordon said, "Hey, what's shaking, MC?"

I wasn't sure about the "MC," so I asked, "MC?"

Gordon and the others at the table started laughing, "Yup, MC – Mad Crapper." I just shook my head and laughed along.

I tried to guide the conversation away from the rumor. "Did you guys get all the trenching and excavation done for the new flow meters? I spent the day down at Chandalar, so I didn't make it to your job today."

Gordon quickly responded, "Yes, sir, Mister MC." I knew that it would be a losing battle to try and converse about anything, so I ate my dinner and kept quiet.

Dinner was done, and I was feeling a little tired as I made the walk back to camp. I was greeted upon my arrival in my room by my roommates. They were lounging on their beds, reading. I grabbed my shave kit, towel, shorts, and a tee shirt and headed down the hall to the communal shower. I always find it relaxing to shower in the evening, and I wouldn't have to fight the morning rush for a shower.

The following morning, the roommates were gone when I awoke, probably showering. I dressed and headed out the door before they returned. When I stepped out the door of the camp, the sky was crystal clear, the moon was bright, and the stars looked close enough to reach out and touch. And then the cold hit me. The temperature must have been -50°F. BRRR! It was going to be a cold day, but at least the wind was not blowing.

I walked to the PLQ for breakfast, my favorite meal of the day. It's difficult to screw up bacon, eggs, coffee, and toast. There were only a few in the dining room this morning, which was normal at 4:30 a.m. Day shift doesn't start until 6:00 a.m., so most get to the chow hall around 5:15 a.m.

I walked through the chow line filling my plate and bowl with fresh cantaloupe, honeydew, crispy bacon, scrambled eggs, sourdough toast, a glass of water, and of course, the largest cup of coffee. I was just finishing eating the last bite of toast when Doug, the boss, sat down at the table across from me.

"Morning, Schuelke, mind if I join you?"

I nodded, "Go ahead."

"I tried to catch you at the end of the day, yesterday, but you had already left the office. I got an update from the Pump Station 1 Asset Team Lead (ATL) regarding our discussion yesterday. All the things that we discussed regarding the damage to your room at Annex 1 were true. The other damage at Pump Station 2 and 3 was not true. And they have concluded with 100% certainty that it wasn't you."

I laughed. "Was there ever any doubt that it wasn't me?"

Doug laughed along with me, "I believed it wasn't you after our conversation yesterday, but others, well, I, er, can't speak for. I know you're headed back to Pump Station 1 today, so when you get to Annex 1, you will have to get a temporary room while they repair the damage to your assigned room."

"Okay. No worries. Can you do me a favor and quash the new nickname that I have been given over this? The Mad Crapper."

Doug laughed. "You know I can try, but this is going to stick for a while, at least until the next rumor flows down the pipeline and there is someone else to make fun of."

And here is the rest of the story…

The guy who was in the room next to me at Annex 1 knew that the room was my permanently assigned room. He assumed the damage done to the room was done by me. Therefore, he was responsible for the start of the rumor mill. I tried for several days to catch him in his room to talk about what he had started but was unsuccessful until one evening after dinner. His door was slightly ajar, so I knocked.

"Come in," he yelled.

I pushed the door open and the look on his face was

priceless. I had never seen someone turn ghost white before, but he did.

He immediately started apologizing, "I'm so sorry. I just assumed that you did all that stuff. I knew that it was your room, and I had seen you around camp that morning. I didn't know you had traveled to Pump Station 4."

I laughed. "Thanks for the new nickname. One day I will repay the favor." We shook hands and parted on good terms.

The damage to the room was done by a guy working for another company. He had been placed in my room temporarily. It wasn't abnormal to use unoccupied permanent rooms as "swing rooms" while the permanent occupant was not there. The individual was terminated by his employer, so in retaliation, he busted up the desk, broke the window, cut-up the bed, and defecated in the room. Lucky for him, I took the brunt of the rumor and was awarded the nickname, "The Mad Crapper."

CHAPTER SIX

WELCOME TO RUSSIA

I had the opportunity to work on an international project during my career in oil and gas. I spent one year working in Calgary in Alberta, Canada where we completed the engineering and then a year in the Russian Far East.

The engineering was nearing completion, and I worked with my employer to make travel arrangements to start working rotation in Russia. The journey would be a long, arduous process and would include planes, trains, and automobiles. I would travel from my home in Anchorage, Alaska to one of two job sites in Russia: Komsomolsk-on-Amur or Sovetskaya Gavan.

The Checker Cab pulled up in front of, and came to a stop at, the international terminal at the Ted Stevens International Airport, located in Anchorage, Alaska. The driver turned to me in the rear seat. "That'll be $8.50." He must have thought I couldn't read the glowing red meter on the front dash.

I handed him a $10 bill and requested a receipt. "Fine. I write you receipt," he stated in broken English.

While I waited for him to complete the receipt – this

was in the days before credit card machines with printers in cabs – I gathered my jacket and briefcase and stepped out of the cab. The weather was clear and cold, probably hovering around zero. I waited for him to pop the trunk to grab my two oversized suitcases. I was told to bring everything I would need for my rotation, including toilet paper. I thought it odd, but I had packed six rolls of Charmin Extra Soft.

The driver exited the cab and walked to the back, receipt in hand. He handed me the receipt and opened the trunk. He reached in and, with a concerted effort, lifted the first bag out of the trunk. The bag was probably almost as heavy as he was; he wasn't a very big guy at all. He placed the bag on the curb, and I reached over and extended the pullout handle. He grabbed the second, this time prepared for the bulk. He set the bag on the curb with a grunt. "Thank you, sir. Safe travels," he said as he headed back to the warmth of the car.

I stacked the two suitcases on top of each other and began the short walk into the terminal. I had never flown out of this terminal; it was older and a bit dilapidated. I wondered if this was the original terminal or just lacked maintenance and upkeep. Once inside, I looked for the Korean Airlines ticket counter. There was only one ticket counter currently open. That must be it.

I thought to myself, "Great. It is going to take an hour to get through the line." There must have been a hundred people already in line. I realized that this was the line for general boarding / economy, and there was a separate line for first and business class. Thankfully, my arrangement allowed me to travel in business class.

"Joh-eun achim-ibnida," the young woman stated and then started laughing after looking up and realizing I was not Korean. "So sorry, sir. Good morning," she apologetically said.

I laughed to myself as I had not really paid attention to the patrons standing in line, but I would have estimated that ninety-nine percent were of Asian descent. "Good morning," I replied. I handed her my passport and the printout of my confirmation number. "What is your final destination with us today, sir?" she asked politely.

"I am traveling to Seoul and then on to Russia," I replied.

"Thank you for flying with us, sir," she responded. And, after what seemed like forever, the ticket began to print. "How many bags will you be checking, sir?" she asked.

"Just two. Thank you. Will they be checked only to Seoul, or will they be tagged to go all the way to Khabarovsk?" I asked.

"Yes sir, they will go to your final destination, even though you are not flying all the way there with us," she smiled proudly.

I placed the two suitcases on the scale and was surprised that both weighed in at forty-nine pounds, just under the limit of fifty before you had to pay extra.

She carefully secured a tag to each bag and handed me my boarding pass and baggage ticket stubs. "Thank you, sir, have a safe flight and a good day," she said.

"You as well. I mean, have a good day too," I laughed.

Check-in was now complete, and it was time for the arduous process of going through the security checkpoint. The rules for flying had recently changed due to the attacks on the World Trade Center and the Pentagon – 9/11, a day that changed the way we travel. The line was long but seemed to move quickly. This was prior to the days of the body scanner, so metal detectors and bag searches were the processes being used.

I began the process of taking everything out of my pockets, taking off my shoes, and removing my belt. I placed my carry-on bag on the belt along with all the things from my pockets and proceeded through the metal detector.

The TSA agent politely said, "I need to look in your bag, sir."

"Go right ahead," I responded.

This is where it got interesting, because as he started to remove the possessions from my bag for inspection, he pulled out my Leatherman still in its case. I thought to myself, "Well crap. There goes $100."

He carefully went through everything, and didn't discover anything, and said, "You're good to go." I was a little perplexed and my Leatherman unconfiscated, but maybe he didn't know what it was.

After gathering my belongings, I re-dressed myself and headed into the terminal. The next order of business was to find coffee and breakfast, and the choices were very limited. I did find Cheerios and milk, a banana, and coffee.

I had about an hour and thirty minutes before the boarding process would start. I was surprised at the number of people waiting in the terminal; there had to be close to 400 people there. I had never been on a plane larger than a 737, so it would be an interesting experience flying on a 747.

I noticed that there were two jetways out to the aircraft, so I knew the boarding process would move quicker but would still take a lot of time. The line to board stretched down the hallway in the terminal, and, overall, it only took about forty-five minutes to seat everyone.

I took my seat in the upper lounge in business class, laid my seat back, and relaxed. After waiting for what seemed like forever, we were pushed away from the gate and taxied out to the runway. The engines revved, and we sped down the run, quickly achieving liftoff speed. Liftoff was smooth, which was abnormal coming out of Anchorage.

We reached 10,000 feet, and the pilot made his normal announcements: estimated flying time, cruising altitude, etc. I reclined my seat all the way back, which was almost completely horizontal, and settled in for the ten-and-a-half-hour flight to Seoul, South Korea. I was just starting to doze off when someone started playing with my shoes. I sat up to find the flight attendant removing my shoes.

"Sorry. We want you to be comfortable. We have slippers. Would you like champagne, sir?" she asked politely.

I thanked her and said, "No, thank you. But if you have orange juice, that would be great."

"Yes, sir. No problem. Would you like pulp or no pulp?" she asked.

"Either will be fine. Thank you," I chuckled in response.

I had never flown internationally but later came to find out that the major air carriers had an unspoken competition to see who treated their customers better in business class. They were hungry for the business, and for the ticket price of $5,500, I understood.

The flight was relatively smooth and uneventful. Therefore, I slept most of the way. I knew that there was a huge time difference, and I would end up with jet lag on the other end, so I tried to maximize my rest time. We landed in Seoul at 9:00 p.m. local time, which was ahead of schedule. I thought to myself, "We must have had a tail wind."

The deplaning process started with the upper deck, which was great since I was seated there. Down the staircase, and out the door first, I walked into the terminal at Incheon International Airport. I was impressed. I did not know what to expect, but it was more modern than most of the domestic airport terminals I had been through in the United States.

I wandered through the terminal, following signs for the Incheon International Terminal. My flight for Khabarovsk, Russia did not depart until the next afternoon, so I would be able to get a few hours of decent sleep prior to the flight. Additionally, the airport terminal closed at midnight, and you had to be out of the terminal or be escorted out by armed military guards.

I checked in at the hotel and found my way to my room. Even though the space was small, the room was well decorated and comfortable. There was a bed, desk, small bathroom and shower, and a television set. After a quick shower, I turned on the television and perused the channels, finally finding the BBC News, which was one of the only channels in English.

I drifted in and out of sleep, my normal sleep pattern interrupted by the time change, seventeen hours difference. I woke around 6 a.m. the following morning and decided I better roll out of bed to make sure I was out before checkout time. I made coffee, took a shower, and packed things back in my bag. After a brief visit to the front desk for checkout, I wandered back into the terminal, which was busy.

I found an open restaurant – there were a multitude of choices – and most offered the menu in many languages. I found an empty table and perused the menu. Nothing looked appetizing. I think it was the lack of true rest and the uncertainty of how good the food might be. I ordered a bacon cheeseburger and fries. It was a brief ten-minute wait for the food to come out of the kitchen. It looked edible.

Although the food was pretty tasteless, it had been seasoned with lots of salt. I ate about three quarters of the burger and about half the french fries before I gave up due to the amount of salt. I would guess that I had achieved my salt intake for a week. I signaled the waitress for the check, which she promptly brought over. After a quick look, I handed her $20 and thanked her.

Upon exiting the restaurant, I looked for a map of the airport so I could determine where I needed to be. After locating a map, I realized that I had a long walk back to the other end of the terminal, almost at the gate where I had arrived. As I walked through the airport, there were many shops for designer brands and quite a few duty-free shops.

I arrived at the gate, and there were about a dozen folks seated in the boarding area. I had about an hour to kill before the boarding process would start, so I found a seat and pulled out my cell phone. Of course, there was no signal, which I am sure was because I had an American cellular provider. "Oh well," I thought. I decided I would sit and people watch, one of my favorite airport activities.

The time seemed to pass quickly, and the terminal had filled with travelers. At exactly 8:00 a.m., boarding time, a robust gentleman exited the office behind the ticket counter. He was dressed in a military style uniform. Even though it was the air carrier's uniform, it looked more military. He had a resemblance to Joseph Stalin, including the thick mustache. I wondered if he was somehow related.

The line quickly formed once the announcement was made, which I didn't understand since it was in Russian. I played the lemming and got in line like everyone else. There were probably seventy-five people in front of me. I pulled out my boarding pass, passport, and Russian visa. The line slowly moved forward.

I was next in line and handed the gentleman all of my

documents. He looked at my passport, at the visa, and then back at me and smiled. He scanned the ticket, looked at me nervously, and scanned it again. After the third attempt, he spoke to me in Russian. I had no idea what he was saying, so I shrugged my shoulders. In broken English he said, "Sir, step to the side."

I did as instructed and watched him board everyone else remaining in the line. After he had boarded the last passenger, he signaled for me to come over. "Sir, your ticket no good," he stated in his best English.

"What do you mean?" I asked.

"Sir, no funds have been received," he responded. I thought to myself, "That's impossible." My employer had purchased the ticket; otherwise I wouldn't have been able to print out a boarding pass.

I didn't want to have an argument and end up being carted off to jail, so I asked, "How much is the ticket?"

He smiled. "It is five-hundred American dollars."

I thought, "Not a big deal. I will just pay for it and include it in my first expense report." I pulled out my wallet and found my visa credit card. I attempted to hand him the card, and he refused the card.

"Cash," he stated.

I pulled out my wallet once again to see how much cash I had. I already knew that I did not have five hundred, but I could go to the ATM. I asked, "Is there an ATM?"

He smiled and said, "No time. How much you have?"

I counted out two-hundred and twenty-six dollars.

"That enough," he said as he snatched the cash from my hand without it being offered. He pointed to the boarding door and nodded. I would later realize after discussions with my co-workers that I had been scammed into giving up my cash.

I boarded the plane and found my seat in first class,

which was one of the benefits traveling on international assignments. Travel was always business class, and, in most cases, that's the same as first class. We sat on the plane for at least an hour before the it was pushed back from the gate. We then sat on the tarmac for another forty-five minutes. After an announcement from the pilot and the safety briefing from the flight attendants, we started our journey to the runway. I did not understand a word of either, as it was in Russian. I wondered if I was the only English-speaking passenger.

I watched out the window as we sped down the runway, quickly achieving takeoff speed. As we lifted off, I watched the landscape below us. I had never been in Korea but thought of my dad who had served several tours of duty here during the war. The city of Seoul was huge. I guessed in the millions of people. It quickly faded into the distance as we flew north towards Russia.

I settled in for the long flight, approximately nine hours. I was excited and nervous about flying into Russia. The Cold War was long over, but I didn't know what to expect being in the former U.S.S.R. I had met a number of the Russian team members while working with them on the engineering in Calgary, but being in their country would be different, or so I thought.

I drifted in and out of sleep during the flight and was happy to hear the pilot announce that we were beginning our descent into Khabarovsk. I did not understand the announcement but did understand the word Khabarovsk. I assumed we were making our approach as the flight crew started their clean-up of the cabin.

It was approximately 7:00 p.m. as we made the approach. I could see lights on the ground as we descended. The lights were spread far and wide, apparently a large city. We descended rapidly, and as we touched the ground, I thought we blew a tire. There was a thump, thump, thump as we sped down the runway.

As we slowed and came to a stop, I peered out the window. I realized the thumping noise was made as we ran over joints in the runway surface. The weeds were growing tall and proud in the joints. I thought to myself, "Do they not do runway maintenance?"

We taxied to the terminal, which had no jet ways. We came to a stop and waited. The flight attendant made an announcement, which I assumed was to remain seated until the doors opened. Again, I spoke no Russian, so I was purely guessing. I waited until others stood and started to gather their belongings. When I made it to the door, I was surprised to see that they had rolled stairs to the door.

We were parked a good two hundred yards from the door into the terminal. "Interesting," I thought to myself. Maybe they were afraid to park too close. I descended the stairs and started the walk across the tarmac to the door the other passengers were entering. I was surprised when I walked through the doors, and there were signs in both Russian and English. I also noticed there were quite a few things that were emblazoned with the Alaska Airlines logo. I later found out that Alaska Airlines at one point used to fly direct to Khabarovsk from Anchorage, Alaska.

I noticed several airport staff wearing military uniforms. I assumed they were the Russian version of American TSA. I stood in line under the sign that said, "Immigration." I pulled my passport and Russian visa from my briefcase in preparation to approach the counter. The first step in the process was to have my temperature taken. The young woman in medical attire made a comment in Russian, the only word I understood was, "Amerikanets."

I proceeded to the counter where the woman asked, "Passport, visa, and what is your business here?"

I handed her my passport and visa and stated, "I work for Exxon-Mobil Nefte Gas."

She looked at my picture, stamped my passport, and handed it back to me. She smiled and said, "Dobro pazhalovat. Welcome to Russia."

I responded, "Thank you." Then I proceeded to walk towards the double doors, which opened into the terminal.

I walked through the doors and into the terminal. There was a large crowd gathered around the luggage carousel that had yet to begin moving. I took the opportunity during the wait to scan the crowd, hoping to see someone with a sign containing my name. There was no one noticeable with a sign. After about twenty minutes, the carousel screeched loudly and began moving. Slowly, passengers and their luggage were reunited. I waited for my bags to appear.

As quickly as people grabbed their bags, they exited the terminal. My bags – the first one, then the second – made their way toward me. I grabbed them from the belt and walked to the open area, still hoping to see someone come in with a sign indicating they were here to pick me up.

A middle-aged man approached me and asked, "Where you go? I take you?"

I thanked him and said, "I have a ride."

I continued to wait for someone to show up and collect me, but to no avail. I was hoping they were just running late or maybe they were waiting outside. I walked outside, and the man once again approached me. "Where you go? I take you?" he again asked.

I repeated, "No, thank you. I have a ride."

I was starting to get nervous, so I walked back in the terminal, which was now empty except for two older women who were frantically mopping the floor. As they completed a section, they were turning off the lights. I searched for a pay phone and found one located on the far wall. I walked over, picked up the receiver, and tried to dial the number for the shipyard. I tried several times, and each time I received an automated recording, which was in Russian, so I had no idea what it was saying.

Now I was seriously concerned. It was now 8:30 p.m., and it appeared the airport was closing. I carted my bags outside and was greeted by the man again.

"Where you go?" he asked again, "I take you, I taxi."

I replied, "Komsomolsk on Amur, Amur Shipyard. How much?"

He thought for a moment and said, "Six thousand rubles. You go ATM." He grabbed my arm and said, "ATM" and started pulling me inside.

There was an ATM inside the doors. I wasn't sure that my American bank card would work but thought, "What's the harm in trying?" The ATM blinked to life, and I was surprised that there were instructions in Russian and English. I selected "withdrawal" and typed in seven, zero, zero, zero. After thirty seconds, the screen read, "Transaction approved." It started to count out one-hundred-ruble notes.

I kept an eye on my luggage sitting outside next to the taxi, which had no signs, lights, or other indications that it was really a taxi. I retrieved the stack of rubles and walked back out to the car. I handed the gentleman the stack of bills, and he loaded my luggage into the back of the small station wagon. He then proceeded to open the back door, push the front seat forward, and stated, "You like. Get relaxed."

I climbed in the rear seat of the car. It was not overly comfortable, but with the seat pushed forward, I could at least stretch out a little. The driver climbed in the driver's seat, started the car, and reversed out of the parking space.

He drove through the parking lot, and we finally exited the airport. We drove through the mostly deserted city and appeared to be heading out of the city itself.

We had been driving for about forty-five minutes through the mostly dark city, and now it was completely dark outside, with no more streetlights. At this point, I began to worry about my safety. I had no certainty about where we were going or about the guy driving me.

The driver turned to me in the backseat and said, "You sleep." This just added to my nervousness.

I did manage to relax enough to drift off into sleep. It had been a long couple of days since starting my journey to my new work location. I was awakened by the car being downshifted and slowing down. We were approaching streetlights. As we slowed, the driver realized I was awake and said, "Coke."

I smiled at the driver and shook my head, "Nyet."

He stated, "You like Coke? I buy." The driver turned off the road into what appeared to be a truck-stop of some kind.

The trucks surrounding the small building all looked foreign and very old. The driver parked the car, shut-off the engine, and looked back at me. "I come back." He opened his door, exited the vehicle, and walked into the building.

My thoughts turned to my nervousness about not knowing where we were. I thought, "Was this the place where they would rob me and leave me stranded?"

Twenty minutes later, the driver exited the building and approached the car. He stopped briefly outside the vehicle and lit a cigarette. After several drags on his cigarette, he flicked the butt to the ground and opened the door. He reached back with a Coke in his hand and said, "You drink."

I thanked him for the Coke as he restarted the car and reversed out of the parking space. We turned back onto the two-lane road and drove into the night.

I watched the scenery, which was mostly wooded, the trees silhouetted by the moon. I wondered where we were and where we were going. The caffeine in the Coke woke me up, and I managed to stay awake for the next two and a half hours. We were approaching what appeared to be a city of some kind. Streetlights were sporadic, unlike most cities in the U.S.A. Most of the city was blanketed in darkness.

I checked the time on my watch. If my math was correct, the time was now 1:00 a.m. The driver turned to me and stated, "Welcome Komsomolsk. Where you go?"

I only knew I was going to the Amur Shipyard, which after several attempts of trying to explain, I gave up. I said, "Hotel." He nodded his head and gave me a thumbs-up.

We drove into the city, and he pulled up in front of a three-story building that was completely dark. He parked in front of the building and shut-off the engine. He turned to me and said, "You wait." He exited the vehicle and approached the building. The double front doors were probably ten feet tall. He began pounding on the doors.

I thought to myself, "That's interesting. Is this a hotel?" Unlike the hotels I am used to, there was no parking lot lights, no visible sign, and no lights on inside.

He tried banging on the door repeatedly, to no avail. After ten minutes of trying, he returned to the vehicle. "No answer," he said. He restarted the vehicle, and we backed out of the parking space. He drove deeper into the city. The city appeared to be decent sized. We pulled up in front of a building that was probably six stories tall. There was one lighted window. He parked the car, turned off the engine, turned to me and said, "You wait." He approached the front doors and started banging on them.

After five minutes, the outside light came on, and someone appeared at the door. They spoke briefly, the door opened completely, and he stepped inside. A few more lights turned on inside. After another minute, he exited the building and approached the car. He opened the door and said, "Three hundred rubles and passport." Thankfully, I had been smart enough to get a few extra rubles. I pulled out my wallet and counted out three one-hundred-ruble notes and handed him my passport.

He took my passport and the cash and said, "You come." I undid my seatbelt and stepped out of the vehicle. It felt good to stretch my legs. I had been in the car for five hours. He went to the rear of the car and unloaded my luggage. He carried my bags into the hotel and set them by the front desk. He chatted with the older woman briefly and handed her the cash and the passport. She looked the passport over, looked at me, and smiled.

She filled out some paperwork, which appeared to be some kind of receipt book. It looked like an old order book used in restaurants back in the States. She ripped the page out of the book and placed it in my passport. She then set them both to the side of the desk. She chatted briefly with my driver and then pointed up the stairs. The driver waved me towards the stairs as he grabbed my bags. He stopped at the bottom of the steps and waited for the woman to approach. She turned on lights as we slowly made our way up the stairs.

I assumed that there was not an elevator, or maybe it was inoperable. We climbed stairs all the way to the fifth floor. We stepped into the dark hallway. The driver and the woman spoke, and then the woman disappeared down the dark hallway. I heard knocking, followed by brief conversation between two people. The woman from the front reappeared with another woman following closely behind her.

The two women and my driver spoke briefly. The front desk woman disappeared back down the stairs, and the other woman fumbled with light switches. The lights in the hallway were now on, and we walked down the once-dark hallway. We stopped in front of a door about halfway down the hallway. The woman opened the door and turned on the lights in the room. The driver stepped in and set my bags by the bed. I assumed he was done and would soon begin his journey back to Khabarovsk.

I thanked him. He stepped out of the room, and he and the woman disappeared down the hallway, chatting the whole way. I looked at my surroundings. The room was about the same size as my dorm room in college. There was an old metal bed frame with a thin mattress, a small desk and chair, a small table with a wash basin and pitcher, and a free-standing armoire.

I wondered if all the hotels were the same. I was surprised there was not a bathroom but figured I would find it in the morning. The only thing I wanted was to lay down and sleep. I would figure out my next step when I awoke. It was close to 3:00 a.m. I just wanted sleep, real sleep, not on a plane, not in a car. I didn't even bother to undress; I just laid down on the bed for much needed rest.

I thought I would fall asleep as soon as my head hit the pillow. Unfortunately, there were too many thoughts in my head. "Where was I? Where was I supposed to be? Why didn't anyone greet me at the airport? Was I forever lost in a foreign country?" I tried my best to put all those thoughts to sleep, but I was over-tired and worried. Eventually, I drifted off to sleep.

I was awakened by the sun shining brightly through the

window. I jumped out of bed. I jumped out of bed in strange surroundings. "Where is the bathroom?" I opened the door into the hallway and peered down the hall. I saw no visible sign indicating a bathroom. I thought, "I better go find the bathroom before I pee my pants." I wandered down the hallway. As I passed a door that had a window, I heard running water that sounded like a shower.

I hoped this was a public bathroom. I knocked on the door, and when no one answered, I stuck my head in the door. There were several sinks and a row of toilets. Yay for me. There was a wall in the center of the room; I assumed the other side was the showers. I used the bathroom and peered around the corner of the wall. There was a gentleman showering. The shower room reminded me of a high school gym locker room.

I wandered back to my room and unpacked my shaving kit and clean clothes for the day. I looked out the window to see if I could see anything. It was a bright, sunny day. There were several buildings, and it appeared I was in a good-sized city. I was hopeful that I was where I needed to be. I walked back down the hallway to the bathroom. I brushed my teeth, shaved, and then took a long hot shower.

Task number one for the day was now complete. Now, I had to figure out where I was and where I needed to be. I repacked my suitcase and headed down the stairs. I was greeted on each floor by a woman, who I later found out was the "floor warden." They are responsible for the tenants on their respective floor. I made it down to the lobby. There was an attractive young girl behind the desk. I hoped she spoke English. She did not. We were at an impasse. I was trying to explain where I needed to go. I even drew a picture of a ship. I thought to myself, "How do I make her understand?" I had a brilliant thought; I knew the company letterhead had both English and Russian.

I returned to my room, unpacked my portable printer and laptop. I printed out a copy of the letterhead. I was proud of my brilliance. I took the freshly printed letterhead back down the stairs to the front desk. I handed the girl the letterhead, pointed to myself, and then pointed at the address on the letterhead. She smiled, nodded, and grabbed the phone.

She carefully dialed the phone number on the letterhead and handed me the phone. The phone rang multiple times and finally a female voice came on the line. She said something in Russian.

I said, "Hello. This is John Schuelke. I work for Exxon-Mobil. Is this Amur Shipyard?"

The voice on the other end said, "Who is this?"

I repeated, "This is John Schuelke with Exxon."

The girl said, "I'm sorry. I do not know you," and she hung up.

I thought to myself, "Great. That did not go as planned. What do I do now?" I handed the phone receiver back to the young woman behind the desk. She smiled and placed the phone back in the cradle. I headed back to the stairs, wondering what my next step would be.

I was about halfway up the first flight of steps when I heard the phone ringing, followed by the young woman yelling, "John, John, John." I turned around and headed back down the stairs. As I approached the desk, the woman was holding the phone out towards me.

I took the receiver from her and placed it to my ear. "Hello, is this John Schuelke with Exxon?" the voice on the other end said.

I responded, "Yes."

"Where are you?" the voice asked.

"I think I am in Komsomolsk, but I am not sure," I stated.

The woman on the other end asked me to put the desk lady on the phone. I motioned for the young woman to take the receiver from me. She slowly placed the phone to her ear. The two women chatted for about ten minutes, and I wondered if they knew each other.

The young woman behind the desk motioned for me to take the receiver. I took the receiver from her and placed it to my ear. The woman on the other end said, "I know where you are. We will send a driver to pick you up. He will arrive in thirty minutes."

I thanked her, excited that I had been found and was closer to being where I was supposed to be! I bounded up the stairs quickly to my room. I was happy, tired, and excited. I quickly packed my belonging, made the bed, and took my luggage downstairs. The floor lady, realizing that I was leaving and struggling to carry all my luggage, helped me carry the bags down to the lobby. Once I had my belongings downstairs, I sat in one of the two wooden chairs in the lobby, awaiting the arrival of my ride.

Almost exactly thirty minutes later, a young man and woman entered the lobby of the hotel. I hoped they were my ride. The woman approached me and asked, "Hello, are you John?"

I am sure the smile on my face was huge. "Yes, that is me."

She shook my hand, as did the gentleman, and said, "Let us go." She went to the front desk with me, and, after a brief conversation, the young woman behind the desk handed me my passport and the receipt.

While we were checking out, the gentleman, the driver, loaded my luggage into the car. As we exited the hotel, the young woman introduced herself, “My name is Marina, I am translator for ASP.”

I said, “Nice to meet you. Thank you for coming to my rescue.”

She laughed and said, “I am no hero.”

I corrected her, “You would be a heroine, not a hero.” Apparently, she did not understand that I was making a joke.

We got into the car and began our journey across town. The city was alive with people, but there was not a lot of traffic. There were a lot of buses that were full of people, and an occasional train trolley. “We will take you to Hotel Gastinitza, and then shipyard,” she said. We drove through the city. It was very interesting. There appeared to be a lot of high-rise apartment buildings and very few houses.

We entered a roundabout and stopped in front of a multi-story building that had a sign over the door. It read, “Hotel Gastinitza.” The driver pulled up in front of the doors and stopped. Marina told me to wait in the car. She and the driver exited and took my luggage into the hotel. After a brief wait, they returned to the car. Once they were back in the car, we backed out and headed down the street.

It was a quick drive to the shipyard, about a mile away from the hotel. The driver pulled up in front of a two-story building outside the gates of the shipyard. Marina turned to me and said, “Welcome to Amur Shipyard. Please come with me.” We exited the vehicle and entered the building. I was introduced to the receptionist and the security guard.

Marina then proceeded to take me down the hallway, stopping at every office and introducing me. When we reached the end of the hallway, we turned around and headed back down the hallway. We had skipped the first office. “I will introduce you to Gregoire. He is the ASP manager,” she said. We entered a large office, and there was a man seated behind the desk, talking on the phone, smoking a cigarette.

We waited patiently while he talked on the phone. He appeared to be angry at the person on the other end of the phone, but since I spoke no Russian, I could not tell. I later found out that Russian is classified as an "angry language." After hanging up the phone, the man stood up and had a brief conversation with Marina. I recognized my name in the conversation, but nothing else.

Gregoire stood-up and approached me with his hand held out. "Ochin prihatna," he said.

Marina translated, "Nice to meet you." They chatted briefly, and Marina turned to me. "He says you are very brave. An American traveling in Russia alone. You have big, how you say, balls." I laughed to myself and thought, "Or stupid."

The follow-up to this story, and what made it a challenge for my arrival: the shipyard had been told that I would not arrive for another week, so therefore, no driver was sent to greet me at the airport in Khabarovsk.

CHAPTER SEVEN

YOU HAVEN'T MADE A CHOICE- RUSSIAN WIFE

My time working in Russia was in 2003-04. It was approximately ten years after the fall of the U.S.S.R. and an interesting time to be in a foreign country. The Cold War was over, the borders were opening, and people were more freely traveling into the former Soviet Union.

Several major oil companies were partnering with Russian companies to explore and produce oil and gas. The Russian companies were open to American partnerships because it allowed them to "steal" the technology to produce oil and gas and learn about making a profit. Many Americans were now traveling to Russia in the effort to grow the industry, with mostly American men in the mix.

One of the cities I worked in had a population of approximately 350,000 people. The ratio of women to men was 7 to 1. I found it interesting and asked one of my Russian counterparts why the ratio was skewed.

As she explained it, "During WWII, many of our men went to fight in the war. Unfortunately, many of them never returned home. This left more women than men, and the number has not balanced out. We lost one third of the population in this city." I took the answer at face value but wondered how that could be true after nearly six decades.

The phone rang at my desk, and I picked up the receiver. "This is John."

The voice on the other end was delayed and very staticky. "Hi John, this is Mike. How are you?" Mike was a manager for the company at which I had previously worked and my boss at one point in my career.

I wondered why he would be calling me. "I'm good, Mike. What's up?"

He laughed because he knew I was never one to beat around the bush. "I'm wondering if you're happy working in Russia? Or if you are ready to leave?"

I thought about it for a second and said, "I hate being away from home all the time, but the money is great. If the money were right, I might consider leaving. It's been a struggle working here."

Mike replied, "Well I'm glad to hear that you're ready to leave. I have an opportunity for you, but it will not pay the same as what you are making there. Are you interested?"

I thought about it for microseconds. "Yes, if the money is right, color me gone from here. Really, the money is secondary. I'm tired of being away from home, and I'm drinking way too much vodka."

He started laughing and said, "Yeah, I hear they love their vodka in Russia. The day rate will be around $750 per day and a 2/2 rotation."

I was in. "That sounds fair and reasonable. I will have to give notice and complete my rotation here. I have a flight scheduled for February 27th, and then I have a surgery scheduled for March 4th. I would be able to start two weeks after the surgery if that works?"

"John, that sounds great. We are excited to have you back on our team. There are several major projects we are planning, and we need you in the field for execution. I'll discuss with the rest of the team and let you know if it is a no go. Great talking to you." Mike hung up on the other end.

I was excited that I would be leaving. I enjoyed the opportunity to work in Russia, to travel to a different place, but it was time to go back to work in Alaska, at home.

I sat at my desk and thought about the letter of resignation that I needed to send to my current employer. I opened the word processing software on my computer and started typing. Ten minutes later, I was standing at the printer, waiting for the letter to print. The seconds seemed like hours. The printer finally came to life and started to print. The paper slowly fed out of the HP LaserJet into the outfeed tray. I grabbed it, gave it a quick proofread, and signed and dated the bottom of the letter above my printed name. I walked over to the scanner, entered all the information to scan it to my computer and hit the start button.

The paper slowly fed into the machine. Unlike the machines of today, scanning technology was still new and slow. After the document fed through the machine and into the outfeed tray, I picked up the paper and walked back down the hall to my office. I logged into my e-mail, and impatiently waited for the scanned document to arrive in my inbox. Time seemed to slow to a crawl. Five minutes. Ten minutes. Finally, at fifteen minutes, the document arrived.

I opened the document to make sure that it had scanned properly. The alignment was off, but at this point, I didn't care. I copied the document to my portable drive, then started a new e-mail to my employer. "Dear Malcolm, it has been a pleasure to work for you, but I regretfully inform you that I will be leaving to pursue a new opportunity. Please find my official letter of resignation attached. John." The words flowed effortlessly, and once the letter was attached, I hit "send."

I sat and stared at the screen for a brief moment, wondering if I had made the right decision. The answer came when one of the Russian managers entered my office. He and I didn't have a great working relationship, we did not see eye to eye, and he typically listened to nothing I said. I thought, "Good decision. I'm leaving and won't have to deal with Vladimir anymore."

After a discussion about several topics, he left my office. My excitement returned, and I had to let everyone know that I was leaving. I left my office and found my personal translator, Lena. "Lena, please come with me. I have news to tell you and others."

She looked at me and said, "What is this news?"

I informed her that I was resigning from my position and would be leaving the project. With tears in her eyes, she said, "You cannot leave. You are nice man and good. I am sad."

I told her that I had an opportunity to go back home and be close to my friends and family. We then proceeded to go from office to office and inform the members of the Russian team that I would be leaving. Reactions were mixed. I had become more than just a mentor, teacher and peer; I had become a friend.

At the end of the day, the head translator, Marina, knocked on my door. "Come in," I announced.

Marina opened the door and stuck her head in. "Vanya, do you have a moment?" (Vanya is one of the translations of John.) I nodded my head and she came in and sat down. “I must talk to you about an important issue,” she said.

I stopped what I was working on and asked, “What’s going on?”

Marina sighed heavily. “You know that I have come to enjoy working with you. I am sad to hear the news that you will be leaving. I want to understand why. The project is not complete.”

I thought carefully about my words and said, “I have enjoyed working here. The project is challenging. And I have made new friends. Russian friends. But it is time for me to leave. I miss my friends and my family.”

“But you do not have a family. You do not have a wife. You are a good man and should have a wife.” She seemed exasperated.

“I am not married, but I have a mother and four brothers. They are my family. I miss being able to visit them. I miss being able to do things with my friends.” I was perplexed by her words and wondered what she was thinking and why.

Her next words made me chuckle: “You have not made your choice,” she said passionately.

“Yes, I have made my choice. I enjoy working here. I enjoy my new friends, but I am ready to be in my home. I have made the decision to leave the project.”

She began to tear up. “But John, you have not made a choice to have a Russian girlfriend to become your wife.” I now understood what she meant about making a choice. She was hoping that I would start dating one of her friends, fall in love, marry them, and take them to America to live a better life.

CHAPTER EIGHT

ARE YOU A WWF WRESTLER?

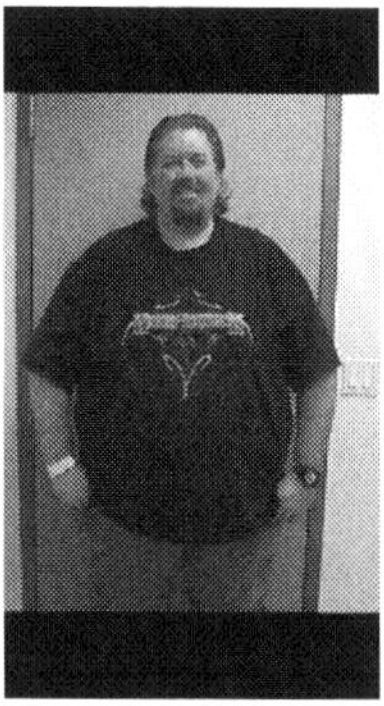

After a beard trim... 1

Let me preface the following story with a description of my physical appearance at the time of the events. I have never been a small man, but at my heaviest I was nearly 500 pounds and at a height of six foot, two inches, I had a large physical stature. I had a full beard and hair down to my shoulders.

There was a knock on my office door. "It's open, come in," I responded.

Marina, the head translator for the shipyard entered my office. "Hello, John," she said with a smile on her face. "John, we have decided to have a party for you. We like to wish you well before you leave us. Would you be okay with that?"

"Marina, of course I would be okay with that. I will miss you all," I said.

"Very well. We shall go to the restaurant this Friday to show you how we send you off to America," she stated proudly. "I shall make a reservation. We will have dinner, drink vodka, and dance into the night. It is Russian tradition," she beamed.

I thought little more of it until later in the day when Marina approached me in the breakroom. "John, we shall celebrate you Friday evening. We shall take you to night club Friday, at 5:00 p.m."

I responded with, "Okay" but thought 5:00 p.m. was early to go to a night club. I did not realize at the time the restaurant also became the night club later in the evening.

Eventually, Friday came, and I was told that a driver would pick me up at 5:00 p.m. to take me to the restaurant. I was also told to dress for dinner and dancing. I was not sure what that meant but figured I would just wear comfortable clothes since I was unsure of what to expect. I worked until 4:00 p.m. and grabbed a ride from the shuttle back to the hotel.

As I climbed the stairs in the hotel to my room, I thought about the evening. I knew that it would be a late evening, and there would be a large amount of vodka consumed. I was glad that we would not be working on Saturday; the impending hangover and lack of sleep would inhibit productivity at work. I showered, brushed my teeth, and donned my best jeans and Harley Davidson tee shirt.

I was sitting in the lobby of the hotel waiting for the arrival of my ride to the restaurant. Promptly at 5:00 p.m., the driver entered the hotel, walked over to where I was seated, and shook my hand.

"John, are you ready for Russian party?" he asked. I

nodded my head, and we headed out the door to the awaiting van. Several of my teammates from the shipyard were already seated in the van. I received greetings from them as I climbed into the first row of seating in the van. The driver started the van, backed away from the hotel, and waited for an opening in the roundabout in front of the hotel. Traffic in the roundabout was heavier than normal, probably because it was Friday evening. There was an opening, and the driver floored the accelerator to get in the flow of traffic.

We drove through the city, and I tried to pay attention to where we were going, but it was pretty hard to remember street names, Russian names. The commute to the restaurant was about fifteen minutes, and, upon arrival, I recognized it. It was the same place I had my first dining experience in a Russian restaurant. The driver pulled up to the front doors of the restaurant, shut-off the engine, and exited the van. He walked around and opened the sliding door, allowing us to exit.

As we exited the van, the driver said, "You have fun. I will wait and take you to hotel after. It is unsafe to take taxi." I thought the comment was odd but remembered that one of my co-workers had been robbed by a taxi driver. I was happy that he would be there to pick us up but wondered if he would be sitting outside, in the van, waiting the entire evening.

We entered the restaurant, where we were greeted by the hostess and one of the translators from the shipyard. We were taken to the main dining room, where a table for thirty people had been set up. The team I worked with was large, but I did not expect them all to show up for the party.

By 5:15 p.m., all thirty seats were occupied. Most of the Russian team had shown up. I was impressed, especially since only part of the American team had chosen to attend. The waitress made her way around the table, taking drink and dinner orders. Of course, the number one drink being ordered was vodka. I knew that tonight was going to be a long night, so I tried to order just water with dinner but was goaded into ordering vodka as well.

What I did not realize was several bottles of vodka had been ordered for the table. When the waitress arrived with several stacks of shot glasses and the vodka, I thought, "Oh no. This is going to be a long night."

Once the glasses were distributed and filled with the first shot, Lena, my personal translator, quieted everyone around the table. "I would like to wish John health and happiness. I will miss you. You have become my friend, and I hope to visit you in U.S.A. someday," she said as she fought to contain the visible tears from falling.

In unison, everyone said, "Nazdrovia." The simple translation is "to health and well-being." The first shot was smooth, and I had become accustomed to drinking vodka, which is nothing like most of the vodka in the States. Vodka is relatively inexpensive in Russia, and there are many varieties: they are either tasty or like gasoline. Several others made toasts, some in Russian, which were translated, or in English. By the time dinner was served to the table, we had finished the first four bottles of vodka with more on order.

The table quieted as everyone ate their meal. Around 7:30 p.m., the tables in the center of the restaurant were being moved to reveal a dance floor. I thought to myself, "That's interesting." They were preparing for the upcoming festivities. Speakers were rolled out from the back and set-up, and once connected, a DJ spoke in Russian and started playing music. Most of the music had a techno-dance rhythm and feel.

At 8:00 p.m., the DJ stopped the music and made an announcement, which Lena told me was to say the dancers would start performing momentarily. Before long, the show started. There was a group of professional dancers that appeared on the dance floor. They performed everything: salsa, jazz, burlesque, and everything in between. They were very talented and entertaining. Their dance routines lasted until about 9:45 p.m. The DJ made an announcement which was translated for me, "All children must now leave the premises."

Lena said, "It is time for the adults to be entertained."

I had no idea what this meant. At 10:00 p.m., a young woman walked out to the center of the dance floor. The music began. She danced solo, and when the next song started, she began to perform a strip routine. "Ah, adult entertainment," I laughed to myself. Several different women performed similar routines for the next hour or so.

When the last woman performed, the dance floor opened to all patrons. I was never comfortable dancing but was dragged out on to the floor several times by the female translators. "John, you must dance. You have no choice; it is your party." I did eventually join in, and I am sure the vodka helped with the inhibitions.

We would dance, return to the table, and drink more vodka. During one of the breaks from dancing, while sitting at the table, I was approached by a rather large man. He was probably six foot-four and all of 350 pounds. He shook my hand and spoke to me in Russian. Lena translated for me, "My name is Vladimir. I would like to have a picture with American."

I laughed and said, "Sure."

After a photo was snapped, he continued to speak to me via Lena. He asked about America, if I liked Russia, if I liked Russian girls, etc. He abruptly ended the conversation and walked away.

Lena told me, "He will be back in a minute."

When he returned, he handed Lena a piece of paper and they spoke briefly. She looked at the paper and handed it to me. I unfolded the paper. There was a name written across the top and what appeared to be a phone number.

Lena said, "This is his daughter's phone number. He would like you to meet her and go on a date with her."

I laughed and said, "Okay, but I am leaving Russia."

Lena and Vladimir continued to chat for several minutes. Vladimir had his back to me, and Lena peered over his shoulder occasionally. When Vladimir walked away, Lena smiled and said, "I have interesting news for you. He would like you to meet and marry his daughter. He would be honored to be the father-in-law of an American WWF wrestler."

CHAPTER NINE

THE HEART SMART DIET - NOT REALLY

I'm not really sure when the American populous started to worry about eating healthy and watching what food they put in their mouth, but the first time I experienced an attempt to encourage oilfield workers to make healthier choices was in the 1990s.

I had been managing projects for an oilfield service construction company along the Trans-Alaska Pipeline. Since we did not work directly for Alyeska, the company responsible for the management of the pipeline, we were required to live in a camp away from the main camps. The main camps were strictly for personnel directly employed by the Company or one of the oil companies. We were second class citizens, so to speak.

The camp I stayed in was referred to Annex 1, the only operating camp left as a remnant of the construction of the pipeline in the 1970s. I'm not sure of the capacity, but there were several hundred people that lived in the camp. Everyone had their own room, but dining, recreation, restrooms, and shower facilities were shared. It was an older facility, aged and worn, but it provided a warm place to stay and hot showers most days.

Even though there was an abundance of food and food choices, the food was mediocre, at best. Yes, there were special meals served, like steak on Wednesday or prime rib on Sunday, but it was usually bland and often overcooked or undercooked. The chow line, much like a high school cafeteria, offered a long line containing multiple choices most meals. For example, the breakfast line usually had pancakes, waffles, biscuits and gravy, scrambled eggs, eggs made to order, bacon, ham, sausage (both patty and link), hash browns, a variety of bread and bagels for toasting, cereal, and milk.

One evening while going through the chow line, there were small signs placed over several entrees and sides. The signs read, "Heart Healthy Choice." I thought it was good that they were looking out for the health and welfare of the workforce. Not everything had to be deep-fried and smothered in butter!

One of my favorite choices for dinner was steamed white rice, chicken, and a salad.

One evening while going through the chow line, one of the cooks was replacing the tray of rice with a fresh batch. I had the opportunity to pass along my gratitude for the healthy choices. "Paul, I'm not sure how you guys are steaming the rice, but it is absolutely the best steamed white rice that I have ever eaten. Can you tell me what y'all's secret is to make it so tasty?"

Paul started laughing, "You know I can't give away our secrets, but I'm glad you like it."

I replied, "I promise not to tell your secret. I just want to replicate it when I go off-shift."

He sighed heavily and said, "Fine. We use butter and cooking oil."

I started laughing, "You can't be serious. That is not very healthy."

He shook his head up and down, "It's the truth. Otherwise, it's just white rice, cooked in a steamer. Just like most of the other heart healthy choices, we have to do something to ensure it has a little flavor and doesn't dry out while sitting under the heat lamps."

The takeaway: just as with most food today, be careful of the choices you make. Even with foods labeled as "healthy," always read the label; you might be surprised to find out it really is not healthy.

CHAPTER TEN

THE CARIBOU CRUISE

There are many regulations placed on the oil and gas industry, including federal, state, and local. The oil companies want and try to be good stewards of the land on which they operate and agree to a multitude of stipulations to lease the land, drill for oil and gas, and then produce product. In all the places that I have worked in the oil and gas industry, Alaska has some of the most stringent regulations. If I remember correctly, there are twenty-six federal, state, and local agencies with oversight of oil and gas activity in Alaska.

There are laws implemented requiring compliance by the oil and gas companies. Some of those laws regard interaction with wildlife. If you have never been to Alaska, there are several areas where oil and gas are produced. There are land-based operations as well as offshore operations. Wildlife includes whales, salmon, sea lions, otters, wolverines, migratory birds, muskox, buffalo, black bears, brown bears, polar bears, arctic foxes, red foxes, wolves, caribou, and moose – just to name a few.

Oilfield workers receive specific training on how to

avoid interaction with the wildlife, as well as training on how to protect themselves from the wildlife. Yes, it is true, a polar bear will hunt you. Workers are also trained how to report an interaction or sighting of wildlife.

This is the story of an interaction between workers and caribou.

I was standing in the chow line, waiting to fill my plate with mediocre food for dinner when I was approached by one of my best friends at the time. We worked in two different aspects of the business. I was in projects, and he was in drilling. "Hey, dude. I didn't know you were on shift," he said as he grabbed my shoulder from behind.

I sighed, "Yeah, I got back a week ago. Only five more weeks until go home day. Doing a couple extra weeks this time. I still don't have an alternate yet. Other than being gone all the damn time, I'm liking the extra dough in the bank account. You never turn down money when they're throwing it at ya'."

He laughed. "Yep. Take it while it's there for the taking. Are you gonna eat in the chow hall?"

I shook my head no. "Naw, I'm gonna go to my room. I'm sick of dealing with people today. And I'm sure if I sit down in here, someone will interrupt MY time."

He laughed. "I'm glad that I'm just a working man and not a fancy manager like you. I work with the same three guys every day. The only time I deal with BS is when the boss is around. Anyway, come by my room before you hit the sack tonight. I wanna show you what me and my crew did today."

I nodded, "Okay."

I returned to my room and ate my dinner in peace. It was a nice change from the day of meetings and dealing with issues, and a good break from people. I figured I had better go visit my friend. Otherwise, he would be butt-hurt. I changed into sweats and headed to his room. His door was closed, but I knew he was in the room. The TV was blaring. It took several attempts banging on the door before he answered.

"Hey bro," he said as he opened the door and waved me in. He looked like he had been asleep. "I'll be right back. I need to hit the head," he said and left the room. Ten minutes later he returned and started fumbling with the VCR, which was built into the TV itself. It was a common setup; it was much easier to move than a TV and a VCR.

He rewound the tape and hit play. The video started out inside of a pickup truck. Each occupant was filmed, and each time the camera switched to someone else, the response was to flip the bird, typical in the oilfield. The video quality was poor, and it was just a video of four guys riding around in a truck, filming the road, the pipelines, and the facilities along the way. This continued for several minutes, and I was wondering what was so cool about this. I had seen everything in person. My buddy said, "Let me fast-forward to the good part."

It was more entertaining watching the sped-up video. He forwarded to caribou everywhere. Obviously, they had encountered one of the herds that migrated across the region. It was not uncommon to see the caribou. The oil industry and the caribou co-existed. The truck slowly drove down the gravel road into the middle of the herd. The caribou moved slowly out of the way of the approaching vehicle.

It was hard to tell how many caribou were there, but I estimated a couple thousand. One of the passengers had rolled down the window and was trying to pet the caribou as they drove by. And as the truck moved through the herd, the camera switched to filming out of the front windshield. Slowly, the caribou, one by one, started to run. The last few seconds of the video were of a lone caribou running down the middle of the road in front of the truck. It ran for probably half a mile before it made an abrupt turn off the road and onto the tundra.

I was flabbergasted by the video. "What the hell were you thinking? You could get run off and thrown in jail for that. You moron."

He laughed. "I ain't worried about it. We ain't gonna get caught."

I shook my head. "How many people have seen this video?"

He said, "Just me and my crew. And now you."

I was irritated that I had been brought into this stupidity. "Destroy the video right now. You know that before long the word will spread, and then you'll be in trouble. And if you don't erase it, I will report it myself."

I waited for him to respond, but he just stared at me until finally he said, "Okay, fine. Here, I'll record over it."

I sat there and waited while he rewound the tape and then recorded over the entire video. I then said, "You're lucky I don't report you; do you know what kind of trouble that video would start? Do not ever do something like that again."

CHAPTER ELEVEN

EMPTY HOUSE - THE ROTATION SCHEDULE

The phone on my desk rang. "Hey, John. It's Bill."

I was surprised Bill was calling. He had just left the day before to go on days off. "Hey Bill, what's up?" I could tell he was in tears, and I wondered what was going on.

"Man, it isn't good, but I don't know if I'm going to come back to work," he said.

"If there's anything I can do, or you need help, please let me know," I replied.

He started to cry, "I gotta go." He abruptly hung up the phone.

I wasn't quite sure what to do, but I was concerned. Bill was normally pretty talkative and didn't hold back. I let it go but was hoping whatever was going on could be easily fixed.

I didn't think much about it until Bill called again. "Hey, John. I wanted to give you a heads-up. I will be coming back to work next week. I will explain everything when I return to work." Bill appeared to be doing better, and I was hopeful whatever was going on was resolved.

The following week, on Tuesday, my office door was

open, and there was a knock. I turned around from my computer to see Bill standing in the doorway. "Come on in."

Bill entered and sat in one of the chairs across from desk. He looked a little tired, but most of us usually looked tired after traveling back to work. It was a joke that we worked harder at home than at work. "Man, the last two weeks have been rough," Bill said.

"Okay. Is everything okay at home?" I asked.

He let out a heavy sigh. "Not really. I went home to an empty house and an empty bank account. Brenda decided after twenty-five years of being my wife, she didn't want to be married anymore. She took everything, even my dog."

I was surprised and at a loss for words. Bill always talked non-stop about his wife, their kids, and all the great things that they did together. I could only respond with, "I'm sorry."

Unfortunately, this is not an uncommon story in the oilfield. The divorce rate is relatively high, 30-50% depending on what statistics you find. I would venture to guess it is probably most common in situations where the spouse is away from home for work. Rotation schedules are hard on families. Often, birthdays, holidays, special events, and firsts are missed because of work.

Some people would disagree and say rotation schedules are perfect for relationships; while you are away at work, your spouse starts to miss you, and while you are home, they start to get tired of you being around all the time.

CHAPTER TWELVE

BEAR BAIT

The pump stations along the Trans-Alaska Pipeline were constructed to pump the oil down the 800 miles of forty-eight-inch diameter pipe. They were strategically placed to maximize the flow from Prudhoe Bay to the terminal at Valdez, Alaska. At the peak of production, over two million barrels per day flowed through the line.

The pump stations were like small towns, containing all the necessary elements to support life. Facilities include water and wastewater treatment, trash incineration, housing, commercial kitchen, vehicle and equipment maintenance, as well as oil and gas processing equipment. The building that contains the kitchen and housing facilities is called the permanent living quarters (PLQ) and was built to house approximately one hundred residents. During times of heavy construction, a portable camp or "fly camp" is used to house additional personnel not permanently assigned to the pump station, but everyone uses the primary dining facility for meals.

The chow line moved slowly for the lunch rush. I wondered what was on the menu causing the slow down.

The line stretched from the start of the serving line to the recreation room, about seventy-five feet. This was abnormal for the lunchtime crowd inside the PLQ.

I waited impatiently in line. I normally had a mid-morning snack, but, for some reason, that day I did not have one. Therefore, I was famished and ready for a hot lunch. I finally made it to the start of the serving line. I grabbed a tray, placed a plate, bowl, cup, and dinnerware on my tray, and inched forward. I had just started construction of my salad when Jackie walked by.

It wasn't abnormal for folks to walk by the line to see what was being served. This time was different for Jackie. She appeared to be stopping and sniffing. I laughed to myself and thought, "Not sure what she is hoping for. It always smells the same." She continued all the way up the line, stopping next to everyone and sniffing.

She then made her way back down the line towards me. I tried my best to ignore her. I was perplexed when she stopped behind me, sniffed, and said, "It's you!"

I turned around with a perplexed look on my face, "What are you talking about?"

She had an angry look on her face. "I knew as soon as I walked in the front door. I smelled something. It's the damned cologne you are wearing."

I laughed and said, "That's interesting, especially since I am not wearing cologne, and I don't even wear aftershave."

Her face reddened and her voice elevated. "We don't wear cologne. We don't wear perfume. All you're doing is bringing the bears here to kill us all!" By the time she finished the statement, everyone in the chow line and dining hall was staring at her and me.

"I'm sorry that you think I'm wearing cologne, but I can promise you that I am not. As a matter of fact, you can go look in my shaving kit, and you'll be surprised: there isn't any in there. Maybe you smell my deodorant?" I said in an exasperated tone.

She glared at me. "You're just bear bait!" she yelled and stormed off.

I never did figure out what exactly she smelled but did find out later that she was a little "off the farm" so to speak. She avoided me like the plague in the ensuing months that I worked there, and I never did see a single bear anywhere near the area.

CHAPTER THIRTEEN

DONUTS, COFFEE, AND A CIGARETTE

The office hallway between the two ATCO trailers is constructed of two-by-fours and plywood sheathing, creating an enclosed walkway, protecting the occupants from the blistering cold temperatures and blowing snow. Located within the fence line which surrounds Pump Station 1 of the Trans-Alaska Pipeline, it's a temporary structure, constructed to house the contracted construction staff responsible for completing a portfolio of maintenance and construction projects along the line. There are eight offices, each measuring eight foot by ten foot.

The window in my office doesn't properly seal, so there is a constant breeze. The office is equipped with a desk, small table, and a not-so-comfortable office chair. The desk has folded-up paper stuffed under one of the legs to act as a shim to keep it from rocking back and forth when you lean on it. The floor is stained, the linoleum is torn in several places, and the trash can is a five-gallon bucket. It is a typical construction office.

"Good morning Jim," I say to the rough and gruff superintendent running the jobs.

"Yup, it's morning," he responds. He drops his hard-hat on his desk, pours a cup of coffee, and heads out the back door to the smoke room, which is now in the lounge of the abandoned permanent living quarters. Alyeska moved all the personnel to the Prudhoe Bay Operations Center (PBOC) just up the road from Pump Station 1. This was done to save money.

Jim and I always competed to see who would arrive at the office first each morning. And our normal morning interaction was about the same. I was always a morning person. I always ate breakfast and drank coffee on the drive to the office. It was rare that Jim would beat me to the office, so I usually had a fresh pot of coffee brewed and waiting for his arrival.

Jim and I worked together on multiple projects and became friends. Our routine was pretty much the same every day. We both arrived at the office around 4:30 a.m. The big difference in our routine was when I arrived at work, I started work, and he started his day.

Jim would walk through the door, hard hat in one hand, mystery brown bag in the other. I learned the brown bag contained one of Jim's essential ingredients for breakfast. There were three things required by Jim to have a good day: coffee, cigarettes, and donuts (which were the contents of the mysterious brown bag). Once he had smoked two cigarettes, consumed two donuts, and had his first cup of coffee, his personality changed, and he was awesome to work with.

Every one of us has different drivers, motivators, and habits. It makes life interesting, and when you start to understand this, it makes the world and people interesting.

Try to figure out what yours and your co-workers' are, and it will definitely help build a stronger, better relationship.

As I side note, I learned that one of Jim's favorite donuts was the apple fritter, so I started bringing them to his office and leaving them on his desk.

CHAPTER FOURTEEN

I LEFT MONEY ON THE TABLE

The oil and gas industry employs millions of people around the world. There are a multitude of ways to be "employed" in the industry. Although the major companies – such as Exxon, BP, ConocoPhillips, Occidental, ENI, etc. – do employ a large number of people, there are an even larger number of people that do not work directly for the Company.

Third party companies supply many of the personnel, processes, equipment, and tools to perform work in the oilfield. You have probably heard the names of those companies: Haliburton, Nabors, Baker-Hughes, Schlumberger, etc. There are also engineering companies: Worley, Parsons, Bechtel, Mustang, Tri-Ocean, URS, etc. And there are companies that provide services such as fabrication or construction.

There are a few with highly technical skills or knowledge that contract directly with the oil companies as consultants. They are typically short-term consultants hired to provide their expertise. I worked with one such individual that was pocketing $2500 per day.

One of the other ways that the oil companies hire expertise is through agencies, often referred to as body shops or headhunters. The oil company will generate a requisition (or request) that is sent to such agencies. The agencies are given a specific list of required job skills and a salary range. The agency does all the work and selects the individual they best feel meets the need. The oil company is not involved in the process directly but has a final say as to whether the proposed individual is acceptable.

I found myself looking at a potential opportunity working through one of the agencies for such a position.

"Hey, Malcolm. This is John. I'm just following up to make sure you received my resume," I said into the phone.

In his thick Scottish accent he replied, "Yes. I received the e-mail and have reviewed your resume. I am waiting for our people to format it into the required format. The Company has a very strict guideline for how they would like to see the resume. I will let you know as soon as it is ready for submittal, and I will send you a copy."

I waited patiently for the next several days to hear back from Malcolm. The phone rang about 5:30 a.m. and woke me from a deep sleep. I tried to wake up but was sure I sounded groggy, "This is John."

It was Malcolm on the other end."Hey, mate. It's Malcolm. I just wanted to let you know I sent your resume forward and copied you. Did I wake you?"

I laughed. "Yeah."

"I'm sorry, mate. I forgot about the time difference between Houston and Alaska. Forgive me?" he said.

I was awake now, excited about the potential to go to work. "No worries. I need to get up and be productive anyway," I said.

"We need to talk about compensation. Do you have an idea what you will want?" he asked.

I hadn't really thought about it, so I just grabbed numbers out of thin air, knowing this would be a negotiation process. "I want $1500 a day, two days paid travel on each end, expenses, and business class tickets to and from work."

He said, "That's reasonable, mate. I'll make the proposal, and we'll go from there. Have a good day. Cheers." And the phone went dead.

Now that I was awake, I started to wonder if I had asked for too much. I guess there was only one way to find out. I would have to wait for a response. I got dressed, worked out, showered, made breakfast, and went about my day. I didn't really think much more about it until later that day. I didn't hear anything back that day. The next day came and went, and I still didn't hear a word. I started to become concerned that I had lost the opportunity.

Finally on the third day, the phone rang, I recognized Malcolm's number. "Hey Malcolm," I said into the phone.

"Cheers, mate. I just received a response from the Company. Congratulations! You will start work next week."

I was surprised they had accepted my terms, with no negotiation. "Thank you, sir. I am looking forward to the opportunity."

Malcolm and I chatted for the next few minutes, talking details of travel arrangements, work locations, etc.

After hanging up, I came to the realization that because they accepted the first proposal, I had not asked for enough. Like negotiating a car deal. When the dealer is eager to accept, you left money on the table.

CHAPTER FIFTEEN

YOU'RE GOING TO GET A LETTER

The time was 6:30 a.m., and my boss walked by my office. As he walked by, he stopped in the doorway. I looked up from the drawings I was reviewing at my desk. "Good morning, Mel," I said.

He replied, "So, you called Mark a dumbass?"

I wasn't sure what he was talking about, so I asked, "What are you talking about?"

"Well, I got a phone call from Helene on Saturday. During the feedback session for the safety assessment, you called Mark a dumbass," he replied. It took me a moment to realize what he was talking about.

One of the tools we used to assess the safety culture within our contractors' teams was the safety assessment. During the assessment process, individuals were asked a series of questions regarding how they would act in various situations. An example of one of the questions is as follows:

"You are performing work and see an unsafe act or work practice. What actions do you take?"

The workshop is a half day process and includes

multiple exercises and questions designed to gauge the buy-in to the safety culture. After the workshop is completed, the data is compiled, and a feedback session is scheduled with the participants and the leadership of that particular company.

During the assessment process for this company, I had compiled the data and scheduled the feedback session. I flew to the site location and met with the participants and the leadership in the theater room of the camp. There were approximately seventy-five people in attendance. One of the topics that was discussed was the expectation to intervene when an unsafe act was observed. Intervention is one of the hardest things that we ask every individual to perform. You are asked to be your brother's keeper and stop them if you suspect they are putting themselves or the facilities at risk.

I was standing at the front of the room and discussing how hard it was to perform an intervention. Mark, their company president was present during the session and seated in the front row.

"Your approach to intervention is going to vary by situation, by individual. For example, I will use Mark. I have known Mark for twenty years, and he used to be my boss. If I see him walking down the stairs, not holding the handrail, I might say something like 'Hey, dumbass. Hold the handrail.' If I didn't know Mark or consider him a friend, I would say something like, 'Hey, buddy. Do me a favor. Hold the handrail.'"

I thought nothing more of my words until Mel asked his question that following Monday. Mel said, "There were multiple phone calls and discussions about the words that I chose. It's never okay to call any company president a dumbass."

I tried to explain to Mel that it was all taken out of

context. It was not meant as an insult, and I was friends with Mark. After Mel left my office, I began to wonder if I was in more serious trouble, but by lunch that day, I had forgotten the whole conversation.

Shortly after lunch, I had a meeting with several of the leaders in our organization, including Mel's boss, Bill. Bill and I were early to the conference room, and we were just talking when the subject of intervention came up. I said, "I learned something about intervention and making sure that I choose the best words, regardless of the situation."

Bill laughed and said, "Yeah, I had several phone calls with Mel over the weekend about that very topic. You're probably going to get a letter from our president."

My heart sunk, "Is it a pink letter? A termination slip?"

Bill started laughing. "No, a letter of thanks."

I was puzzled. "What do you mean? A letter of thanks for what?"

Again, Bill laughed. "A letter saying thank you for saying what several of us were thinking but couldn't say."

I learned a valuable lesson from this incident. I worked diligently to select better descriptions and words when having discussions that may be taken out of context.

CHAPTER SIXTEEN

WHAT'S IT LIKE TO BE A MILLIONAIRE?

There is a misconception regarding everyone working in the oil and gas sector: we are all multi-millionaires. I wish this were true, but it is far from true. Yes, wages are good for the most part, but I know individuals that perform "grunt" work for a little better than minimum wage. There is a small percentage of the workforce in oil and gas earning a seven-figure wage.

With the reward of good pay is the risk of no pay. The oil industry has a cyclical nature. When the price of oil is low, it's a bust; when the price of oil is high, it's a boom. Someone that can survive the cycles will typically end-up with a decent retirement. Not everyone working in the industry is so fortunate. Gone are the days of going to work for a company and expecting to be gainfully employed for a lifetime career. Companies are no longer loyal to employees, and employees are no longer loyal to companies.

The following story is one of those stories about the misconception of being paid millions of dollars...

I was sitting at my desk when Lena and Yuri

approached. They were laughing, smiling, and joking with each other in Russian. Lena was one of the translators assigned to the project to accompany Yuri and provide translation services. Yuri spoke some English but rarely used it. In his words, "I feel stupid trying to speak."

"Good morning, Mister John. How are you this day?" Lena asked.

I smiled and said, "I'm great. How are you and Mister Yuri?"

She laughed. "We are fine. How you say? Like frog hair." It was funny to hear her try to use English.

"Yuri would like to ask of you some questions. Do you have time?" she asked.

I nodded. "I always have time for him. What questions can I answer for you?"

Lena and Yuri chatted in Russian briefly. Lena turned to me. "He would like to be informed of how you feel to be a rich man."

I didn't understand what she was asking. "What do you mean?"

They chatted again in Russian, and she asked, "He would like to be informed on being a millionaire." I still failed to understand the question.

"Does he want to know how to become a millionaire? Is that what you are asking?" I said in response.

They chatted again and Lena said, "We will return in a moment."

They walked out of my office and down the hallway. About fifteen minutes later they had returned and were standing in the doorway to my office. Lena spoke up, "I think I now understand his question. He wants to know how you feel, being a millionaire."

I chuckled at the statement. "I am far from being a millionaire."

Yuri reached, pulled a pen out of his shirt pocket, and said, "Paper." I assumed he wanted a piece of paper, so I pulled out my notebook and opened it up to a blank page. Yuri carefully thought and then wrote the following in over-sized characters, "400 US $." And then pointed at himself.

I assumed the number was what he was getting paid per day and thought, "That's a decent day rate."

I asked Lena, "Is that what he gets paid daily?"

She translated, and Yuri quickly responded, "Nyet, Nyet, Nyet."

They spoke to each other, and I heard the word month. They continued to speak, and eventually Lena stated, "He makes that every month. It is his salary." My heart sank. I did not know if that was a good wage in Russia or not. I assumed because he was a manager, it was a good wage.

After the conversation ended and they left my office, it donned on me. He must have found out that I was making $1,500 per day and therefore assumed that I was a millionaire. I later found out, while working in Russia, that the average wage earner in the shipyard made the equivalent of about $2 per hour. It was easy to understand how Yuri could think that I was a millionaire, if he had discovered what I was getting paid.

CHAPTER SEVENTEEN

ONE DAY WHEN YOU GROW UP

The oil industry employs millions of people in many facets of the business. Depending on your perspective, the money is way too much for a young individual. Wages are typically in line with the skill set of the individual. I have heard rumors and rumblings of welders making several hundred thousand dollars per year in West Texas. I have never met a welder making that much, but they are well compensated.

The downside of a young workforce making good money: they don't always make the best decisions with their money. Often, they are worried about buying a new truck, a snow machine (or snowmobile, depending on where you are from), a boat, an ATV, an airplane, or a motorcycle. Yes, those are great toys, but in the grand scheme of life, toys won't always make you happy. Keeping a roof over your head, food on your table, and clothes on your back will make you happy.

This is a story about three young gentlemen, making a decent wage...

The flight took off on time from Kuparuk, 3:30 p.m. on

the dot. I sat back, closed my eyes, and tried to relax. Unfortunately, my relaxation was interrupted by the three young men seated in the row in front of me. They were a little loud and obnoxious. I am guessing, by the conversation, that they worked for one of the drilling companies operating on the North Slope and were probably roughnecks or roustabouts.

They all appeared to be in their early 20s. "Man, the Company man was being a real douche this hitch. He rode my ass the whole time. I'm surprised that he didn't show up in my room to continue riding me."

The other two laughed, and both agreed. The guy sitting in the aisle appeared to be the senior guy in their trio and was also the most boisterous. "I'm ready for time off, so I can go fish and get fucked up," the guy seated at the window said.

"Yeah, I'm gonna drink beer and ride the Harley. We should hook up and go for a ride," responded the aisle guy.

"I gotta put my new pipes on. Then we can go for a ride," stated the window guy.

"We should all go for a ride. Oh, wait. You ain't got a Harley," the aisle guy said to the young guy seated in the middle. They all laughed, the guy in the middle reluctantly.

"Yeah, one day when you grow up, you'll get yourself a Harley. How many hitches you done? I bought a Harley my second hitch," window guy stated proudly.

I tried to ignore their conversation but was interested when they started talking about motorcycles. I am a motorcycle guy and love riding two wheels.

The guy in the middle said, "This is only my first hitch. I need to save some money before I buy anything."

I thought to myself, "Good for him; save that money.

The aisle guy laughed. "It's okay. You'll figure it out. Harley's all come with women."

I sat listening to these three young men banter back and forth for the next twenty minutes. The conversation always returned to similar comments about "one day when you grow up, you'll get a Harley." I was happy that the guy in the middle refused to give in to the constant ribbing about not having a Harley. They made it sound like the entire world revolved around owning a Harley.

I had finally had enough of their banter, belittling and berating the guy in the middle. I sat forward and said to the guy in the middle, "I think it's great that you are saving money. I also think it's great that your buddies own Harleys. I also think that one day, when they grow up, they will own six, like I do." Needless to say, the trio fell silent. Maybe they had started the process of growing up.

CHAPTER EIGHTEEN

I FOUND IT ON THE GROUND

The radio crackled, "Rob do you copy?" Silence. "Rob this is security. Do you copy?" Silence. "Rob, this is security. Do you copy?"

Finally, after several minutes, a voice on the other end of the empty airwaves, "Go for Rob."

"Rob, this is the security captain. Please call me. It's urgent." The radio returned to silence.

Rob, rather than going to his office to call, drove to the main camp where the security office was located. The distance between the two buildings was about 1,000 yards. He parked outside the entrance and sat in the truck momentarily, wondering what was going on. He placed the truck in park, turned off the ignition, and undid his seatbelt. As he exited the vehicle, he thought to himself, "Which one of my guys screwed up this time?"

He entered the double doors and climbed the dozen steps inside the arctic entry. He opened the interior door and walked the ten steps to the security desk. "What's up?" he asked.

The guard behind the desk said, "Dennis needs to see you. Do you know where his office is?"

Rob nodded and went back into the main hall. He started the short walk to Dennis' office but made a detour into the chow hall to grab a cup of coffee.

After filling his coffee cup, adding sweetener and creamer, he resumed his walk to Dennis' office. As he approached the door, he noticed someone sitting on the chair in the hallway. It was Tommy, one of the guys on his crew. "Hey Tommy, what's going on man?" he asked.

Tommy looked at him. "I'm not really sure, but I was pulled off the job and brought here. I was told to sit here, not leave, and wait for my foreman to show up."

Rob was now more perplexed than after being summoned to the security office in the first place. He knocked on Dennis' door.

Dennis waved him in. "Please close the door behind you."

Rob did as instructed. He took a seat across from Dennis. "What's going on with Tommy?"

Dennis, in his normal soft-spoken demeanor, said, "We have called the state troopers. We have reason to believe that Tommy is in possession of an illegal substance."

Rob was in disbelief. "He's one of the best guys on my crew. What kind of substance?"

Dennis thought for a second. "Someone reported that Tommy has marijuana."

"Come on. Really? I don't believe that," Rob responded, sounding dejected. "Who called?" he asked.

Again, Dennis sat looking at Rob. "I'm not at liberty to say. You know how these things go. We have to investigate, regardless. Once the state troopers arrive, we will search him, his room, and his work area."

"When will the troopers be here? He needs to get back

to work. We have a schedule to meet," Rob stated, sounding dismayed and irritated.

"I contacted the troopers as soon as I received the phone call, so they should be arriving in the next thirty minutes or so," Dennis stated.

Rob sat in silence for several minutes. "I guess we'll just have to wait. This is total BS. Probably one of his buddies playing a joke on him."

Dennis looked at him. "I hope for his sake it is a joke, but if it isn't, he's in a lot of trouble. Please stay around the camp, and I'll call you on the radio when the troopers arrive."

Rob stood and opened the door to exit Dennis' office. As he walked back into the hallway, Tommy spoke up, "Hey bro, what's going on?"

Rob looked at him. "Sorry, I can't talk about it. I'll be back in a little while."

Tommy seemed to be shocked by the statement but went back to staring at the walls as Rob walked down the hallway. The next forty-five minutes seemed to last for days.

Rob's radio came to life. "Rob this is Dennis. Please return to my office."

Rob was sitting in the TV/movie lounge waiting for the call. "On my way," Rob responded.

As he turned the corner into the hallway, there were two state troopers standing in the doorway of Dennis' office. Tommy sat in the chair in the hallway, now looking worried and nervous. Rob walked up to the two troopers and introduced himself, "I'm Rob, Tommy's supervisor." They all exchanged names and entered Dennis' office and closed the door.

Dennis spoke up, "Tommy, sitting out there, was reported

to be in possession of marijuana. We will have to search him, his room, and his work area." Rob just listened and nodded in agreement. There was nothing he could say at this point. Dennis asked, "Rob, can you have Tommy come in?"

Rob opened the door. "Tommy, please come in." Tommy stood, straightened his clothes, and walked into the office.

Dennis asked, "Can you shut the door please?"

Tommy looked really worried. "What's this all about?"

One of the troopers spoke, "Son, we have reason to believe that you are in possession of a controlled substance. We need you to empty your pockets."

Tommy stared at Rob. "This is bullshit. I don't got nothing."

Tommy started to turn red, on the edge of overreacting. "Fine!" He slowly removed his wallet, keys, a pocketknife, and a notepad. "That's it. Nothing there to see. Y'all happy now?" he stated in a matter-of-fact manner.

The trooper once again spoke, "Sir, I will need you to place your hands on the wall above your head. I will need to pat you down and verify that your pockets are empty."

Tommy turned around, faced the wall, and then slapped his palms on the wall. "Have at it!" he said, anger in his tone.

The trooper began the process of patting him down. First his arms, then his neck, chest, abdomen, and lower back. And when he patted down his pockets, he felt something. "I'm going to reach into your pocket. Is there anything in there that will cut or poke me?"

Tommy, sounding extremely irritated, " Nope."

The trooper reached into his left, front pocket. As his hand exited the pocket, it was evident what was in his hand. The trooper held up a neatly rolled marijuana joint, “Care to explain what this is son?”

Tommy looked at it, rolled his eyes, “I found that on the ground. It ain’t mine. I was gonna turn it in at the end of my shift.”

At that point, the troopers asked Rob and Dennis to please leave the office, “We will need you guys to exit. This is now a criminal investigation.”

Dennis and Rob exited the office. The troopers remained in the office for the next hour and finally exited the office with Tommy in handcuffs. “Thank you, gentlemen,” one of the troopers stated as they walked down the hallway with Tommy in tow.

I heard that Tommy never wavered from his story of finding the joint on the ground. Regardless, he lost his job and the potential of returning because of his possession of an illegal substance.

CHAPTER NINETEEN

MOM DIDN'T KNOW

The oilfield, like many places, is a drug-free workplace. In addition, depending on location, alcohol is also strictly prohibited. The North Slope is one such place. The owner-operators of the oilfields on the North Slope prohibit the possession and use of alcohol in their camps.

There are many stories of workers attempting to smuggle alcohol into the camp. They may not make it public knowledge and only consume it their room, but eventually, they get caught. False bottoms have been built into toolboxes, vodka has been injected into mouthwash bottles, and bottles of alcohol have been relabeled. These are just a few of the many ways that smuggling has been attempted.

This story involves an unknowing parent, or so the story goes...

The owner-operators of the oilfields had their own fleet of aircraft to transport personnel and goods to the operating locations. The aircraft used are Boeing 737s. Smaller aircraft are operated within the field, but the 737s provide the main method of transportation from Anchorage to one of two remaining operating airstrips.

There is one operating airstrip in Deadhorse, Alaska, which most refer to as Prudhoe Bay, and the other operating airstrip is in the Kuparuk Oilfield. The difference between the two strips is the one in Deadhorse is paved, and the one at Kuparuk at the time was not.

The Shared Services Aviation Group (shared ownership /operation of the aviation services) was in the process of upgrading aircraft. The 737-200s were reaching the point where maintenance costs would continue to increase, and parts would become more scarce, so a decision was made that newer aircraft would be beneficial. The downside to the new aircraft was that the new aircraft would no longer be able to land on a gravel runway. Boeing, at one point, had manufactured a kit for the 200 series, making it capable of landing on gravel. Boeing did not, and would not, manufacture such a kit for the new 700 series.

In order to continue to use the airstrip at Kuparuk, the decision was made to pave the runway. It was a two-year project because of the weather conditions required for paving.

During the second year of construction, an alcohol smuggler was caught.

The phone rang at the construction superintendent's desk. "This is Steve," he stated.

The voice on the other end responded, "Steve, this is security. We need you to come over to KOC (Kuparuk Operations Center). We have a package that was flagged during the x-ray process."

Steve shook his head. "Okay, I'll head that way." It was normal for all bags and parcels to be x-rayed both coming into and going out of the facility.

It is a short drive, approximately ten minutes from

where the construction offices are located at KIC (Kuparuk Industrial Complex) to KOC. Steve grabbed his hard-hat, safety glasses, and jacket and headed down the stairs and out the front door of the offices to the gravel parking lot, where his company truck was parked. After completing his 360 degree walk of the truck, he climbed in, buckled up, and backed out of the parking space.

As he started the drive, he wondered what had been seen in the x-ray machine. After the brief drive to KOC, he parked and exited the truck. It was a little breezy, and the wind had a chill. Even though it was summer, the temperatures weren't normally warm like most places in the summer.

He entered KOC, stopped at the restroom then the spark room (break room) for coffee, and then went to the security desk. The officer on duty instructed him to go to the baggage room downstairs.

He headed down the stairs and walked into the boarding area where passenger IDs and tickets were checked, and screenings occurred. The officer working the area escorted him around to the x-ray machine, where the officer placed a medium-sized package on the conveyor and ran it into the machine. The image on the screen showed multiple large bottles in the box.

Steve shook his head and asked, "Whose name is on the box?" The officer retrieved the package and read of the name. Steve said, "Yep, that's one of the guys working for the paving company. I'll call their manager."

The paving company's manager answered after about ten rings and sounded out of breath when he answered, "Hello."

Steve proceeded to explain what was going on and told the manager to come with the employee to security at KOC.

The manager said, “It may take a while. I need to pull him off the job but will do so.”

Steve indicated, “Okay. Just get here as soon as possible, and do not tell the individual what is going on.”

Forty-five minutes later, the manager and the individual arrived at KOC and went to the boarding area, where Steve and the security officer were seated in the back office. The officer invited them both back and asked them to have a seat. The officer explained that a package with the individual’s name on it had been flagged during the x-ray process. “Potentially, there is contraband in the box, and you will need to open the package in my presence,” the officer explained.

The employee listened intently, rolled his eyes at the comment, and said, “Okay, whatever.”

The security officer handed him a smart blade to open the box. Everyone in the room watched with curiosity as the employee cut the row of tape on one end, then, the other, and then finally down the seam in the middle. He handed the blade back to the security officer. “Here ya’ go.” The employee then proceeded to fold back the flaps of the box.

To everyone’s surprise, it was filled with packing peanuts. “Let me get a trash bag. I don’t want those stupid things all over the place,” the security officer said. He left the office momentarily. As soon as the door closed, the employee said, “This is a bunch of crap. Isn’t it illegal for them to screen my mail?” The manager explained, “No. You are on private property.”

The security guard returned with a fifty-five-gallon liner. “All I could find was little bitty trash bags, so this will have to do.” He held the bag open. “Go ahead and scoop them peanuts out.” The employee slowly removed handfuls of the packing peanuts, being careful not to send them sailing around the room. The more he dug into the box and removed peanuts, the more the contents of the box were revealed.

There were several half-gallon jugs of alcohol. The employee tried to act surprised. "What the hell, mom? She must have sent this for my birthday."

The manager spoke up, "You realize that you have violated the policy regarding alcohol, and we are going to terminate your employment?"

The employee responded, "Look where that package came from. It's from my mom. She don't know we can't have alcohol."

Post Incident:

The employee was terminated immediately and removed from the site. He never wavered from his story that his mom sent the alcohol. The interesting thing was his mom had the mailing address, which was not public, and his birthday was months away.

CHAPTER TWENTY

WHAT'S IN THAT APPLE?

"Kuparuk security, this is Kris…Uh huh. Okay. I'll activate an emergency response team." He hung up the phone and then dialed the number for the MERT (Medical Emergency Response Team), "This is not a drill. We have an emergency at KIC (Kuparuk Industrial Complex). I repeat, this is not a drill. We have an emergency at KIC." The system activated the pagers of the medical team, including fire and ambulance.

As quickly as individuals could react once the page was received, the team was assembled at the Kuparuk Fire Hall. Gear was donned, and personnel loaded into the ambulance and fire truck. The fire truck and ambulance rolled out of the garage, lights flashing and sirens going. They headed to Spine Road and then turned towards the cutoff road for KIC. Even though the team practiced drills to be ready, real response events were a rare occurrence.

The drive to KIC was a quick five minutes. Upon arrival on the large gravel pad that housed camps, auto repair shops, industrial repair shops, construction offices, materials storage, and fabrication shops, the response team stopped at the Sharktooth Camp, where the call had originated. The security officer in the camp directed them to the chow hall.

Seated in the chow hall was an individual along with one of the other security guards who was also an EMT. The other EMTs, carrying several gear bags, approached the two seated at the table.

The EMT who had been seated pulled the incident commander to the side as the other EMTs began their checks of the patient. "They found him wandering around outside. He appears to be disoriented. His speech is slow and slurred. He doesn't appear to have been drinking, but I'm not sure," the EMT stated.

"Thanks. We'll take it from here," the scene commander said. The EMTs continued to check vitals: blood pressure was normal, heart rate was normal, pupils were dilated, etc.

Several minutes had passed when they declared, "The patient is stable for transport." The patient was walked to the ambulance by two of the responders. He stepped into the back of the ambulance on his own and appeared to be completely out of it.

With the patient loaded in the ambulance, they headed back to KOC (Kuparuk Operations Center) where a full medical facility existed. The medical facility was equipped to treat all emergencies and had a direct phone line to the hospital in Anchorage. The patient was taken into the clinic, where the residing physician's assistant began a more thorough examination.

Based on the description given to the PA, he suspected it might be low blood sugar, maybe diabetes, but wouldn't know until he did blood work. Blood was drawn and a urine sample collected. After negative tests for low blood sugar, and no indicated diabetes in the individual's personal medical record, the PA was perplexed.

"Hi, doc. This is Gary at Kuparuk. I have a patient, and I cannot figure out what is going on with him." He ran through the list of symptoms.

The doctor on the other end thought for a minute. "Do you guys have the ability to drug test? More specifically, can you test for spice?" Even though "spice" (a dubious mix of plant material and synthetic chemicals) was legal to use in the public sector, it was prohibited in the oilfield.

"Yes, we just recently received the test kits. This will be my first one," Gary said. "I'll test, and then we'll go from there. Thanks for your help." After hanging up, Gary proceeded to perform the test for spice, which came back positive.

Gary contacted the security captain to inform him of the positive test. The captain then contacted the individual's employer and asked him to meet at the security office.

Bubba arrived a few minutes later at the security office, where he was greeted by the captain. "One of your employees was brought into the clinic and, during treatment, was tested for Spice. His test came back positive."

Bubba just shook his head. "Dang it. He's a hard worker. I'll get him transported off the slope."

The individual was terminated and removed from the slope on the next available flight to Anchorage.

After he tested positive, the individual's room was searched. During the search, one of the security officers accidentally knocked the apple sitting on the desk onto the floor. When the apple hit the floor, the top came off. The apple had been cored out and turned into a pipe. The spice was located hidden in a bag in the closet.

CHAPTER TWENTY-ONE

CAN I HAVE YOUR DRINKS?

The oil companies in Alaska share transportation services to the oilfield, which is located on the North Slope. Flights originate in Anchorage and terminate at one of several different locations in the oilfield. The distance is approximately 625 miles, and the flights take about an hour and thirty minutes.

Flights traveling northbound to the oilfield are usually somber and docile. I think there are a combination of factors: very few people are excited to go to work; some are tired from working in their time off doing all those "honey-do" projects; some are hung-over from partying all night, knowing they will be without alcohol for an extended period of time; others are just quiet people.

Flights traveling southbound are usually a little more lively. The liveliness is probably related to a multitude of factors: people are excited to be heading home to the important things in their lives – hobbies, friends, and family; people are sharing stories of what went wrong this hitch; people are talking about the plans for their rest and relaxation (R&R); they are able to consume two drinks on the plane home.

The two-drink policy evolved over time and was implemented to protect individuals, as well as the companies they work for. In the "good ol' days," the flight home was lively and entertaining, and there was no limit on the amount of alcohol you could consume, other than the flight time.

On one particular flight home, I had one of my most memorable experiences, and it may have influenced a young man's life to do the right thing…

It was always interesting on "go home day" to watch the behavior of people getting ready to leave for R&R. You could usually tell when someone was going home that day. Their attitude was a little more upbeat. They cared, but they didn't. And in many cases, folks dressed in something other than the fire retardant apparel required in the facilities, construction sites, or drilling rigs.

People would start gathering in the chow hall, TV lounge, and boarding/waiting area sometimes hours before the flight. It was about an hour before boarding time, and I sat in the chow hall talking with one of my employees. The intercom came to life, "We are ready to begin boarding Flight 452 to Anchorage."

I finished my conversation with Dave and gathered my things to go stand in line to board the plane. The intercom chimed and came to life, "Final boarding call for Flight 452 to Anchorage." I thought to myself, "Wow, that was quick. Must not be a full flight today."

I wandered down the stairs to the boarding area. I was surprised when I turned the corner and there were still fifty people standing in line. I usually tried to wait until most of the line was gone before I would join the line. It didn't make sense to be the first one out to the plane. You would have to sit while the buses made trips out to the plane with passengers. Sometimes a forty-five-minute process.

I waited until the line was down to about ten people before I walked over and stood in line. One by one, passengers had their ID and tickets checked and then went through security (which followed TSA guidelines for screening).

"Hey, John. Didn't you just get here yesterday?" Tony asked as he checked my ticket and ID.

"Yeah, it was a long hitch this time," I laughed. I hadn't worked a regular rotation schedule in years, but as a manager, I made frequent overnight trips.

After my normal wanding with the handheld metal detector, I was released to grab my things and proceed to the bus. I always set off the metal detector with my new knee. There were four passengers behind me, the last to board the bus and then the plane.

The plane was full, and there was a young man seated in the middle next to me. I chatted with one of my peers as I removed my tablet from my backpack and stowed my stuff in the overhead bin. I usually slept or read on the short flight home.

The flight crew completed all their pre-flight checks and safety briefing. We taxied out to the runway, waited a brief second, and then raced down the runway before becoming airborne. It was a little bumpy during take-off; must have been some wind. As we climbed to cruising altitude, I had become engrossed in the book on my tablet, so I didn't really pay attention to the announcements being made.

Apparently, they made the announcement about starting beverage service. The young man seated next to me asked, "Hey buddy, are you gonna get your two drinks?"

I explained to him that I had to go into the office. Therefore, I couldn't have a drink.

"That's too bad. If you ain't gonna have them, if I give you the eight bucks, would you buy them and give them to me?" he asked.

I was a little surprised that he asked the question. "Sorry, no."

He looked disappointed. "I'll give ya' the money. It ain't no big deal."

I chuckled. "Yeah, it is a big deal."

He didn't stop, "It ain't that big a deal. You ain't out nothing."

I tried my best not to seem irritated, but I was. "Do you know why there is a two-drink limit? It's in place to protect you, me, and everyone on this plane. It's also to protect your employer and mine. I won't risk my job and break the rules so you can have two extra drinks. And on a personal note, let me give you some advice. Before you ask someone to break the rules for you, you should probably know the person you are asking. I happen to be a manager for ConocoPhillips."

The look on his face was priceless. "I'm really sorry, sir." I believed I made my point, especially when the flight attendant approached our row and asked if we wanted anything. He didn't even order the two drinks he was entitled to buy for himself.

CHAPTER TWENTY-TWO

DO YOU THINK I'M STUPID?

From a young age, human beings will push the limit, just to find out what the limit is. Sometimes, they push too hard and learn the hard way what the limit is. This story is about a young man who tried to push the limit.

The flight from Kuparuk to Anchorage was full, as was the case on most flights. The plane departed Kuparuk and was at cruising altitude when the announcement was made that drink service would begin momentarily.

"We will start beverage service soon. We have Coke products, juice, water, coffee, and beer, and wine. Beer and wine can be purchased for $4.00 each. Please have exact change," the announcement said. Passengers, began their search for cash, digging out wallets and purses to have their money ready. Most passengers enjoy the two-drink maximum, after not being able to drink for a couple weeks.

The flight attendants divided the drink service into three areas. The first cart started at Row 1, the second at either Row 7 or 8, and the third at Row 15. I was seated in my assigned seat, 7D and was one of the first served. I typically had either water or coffee because I usually had work to do when we landed.

The front cart slowly made its way down the aisle, serving beverages and a choice of peanuts or Biscoff cookies. When it reached Row 6, Tonya asked, "Can I get you anything?" The young man seated there proudly said, "Crown and Coke." Tonya said, "I'll need to see your ID." The guy looked too young, and I was glad that she asked.

The guy reached under the seat in front of him and pulled out his backpack. He rifled through the bag, not once, but twice. He then proceeded to check all his pockets. He didn't produce an ID and finally said, "I must have put it in my checked bag."

Tonya just stared at him for a few seconds. "You had to have an ID to go through security. There is no way that you put it in your checked bag. You are lying to me and are underaged. Do you think I'm stupid? I am not going to report you, but I will be watching for you and will let the other flight attendants know."

I was surprised that someone underaged had tried to buy alcohol, and really surprised at the manner they tried to do it. After the flight attendants had completed serving everyone, I left my seat and approached Tonya. "Good job catching that guy. I know you said you would not report him, but if he's willing to break the rules on the plane going home, he is willing to break the rules at work. And, honestly, I don't want guys like that working in the field."

I am not sure if she ever reported the individual...but she is definitely not stupid!

CHAPTER TWENTY-THREE

DIRTY DISHES AND A START-UP DATE

During exploratory drilling in 1994, a discovery was made west of Prodhoe Bay, even further west than Kuparuk. It was across the Colville River and close to the National Petroleum Reserve. At the time of discovery, it was determined to be economic, meaning that it could be developed and produced for a reasonable return on investment. This became the Alpine Field. The field went from discovery to production in a short 6 1/2 years, which, at the time, was the shortest time on record for the North Slope.

I started working on the Alpine project shortly after the engineering started. I was involved in some of the early planning and moved to the fabrication of the facilities being constructed in Kenai, Alaska. It was the first time in Alaska history that sealift modules would be fabricated in Alaska. Most major fabrication for the sealift modules occurred in fabrication yards along the Pacific Rim.

Once the fabrication was completed for the Alpine Central Facility (ACF), I started working on planning and fabrication of the next drill site to be installed at Alpine,

CD-2. I was based in Anchorage, Alaska. Late in spring of 2000, I was asked to travel to the North Slope, specifically to Alpine, to assist with the installation efforts. The construction team was struggling to set and meet realistic targets.

I spent several weeks traveling back and forth to Alpine, trying to understand where the project was, where the problems were, and what it was going to take to bring production into the facilities. At the completion of my efforts, along with several of my peers, I assembled a report that would be sent to senior management. At the time, I reported to the Arco Alpine business manager. I sent him the only copy of the report for review.

He called me the following day and asked if I had any concerns with the report being sent "upstairs."

I told him the report only contains information that I personally verified. There was no opinion, just data, facts, and figures. "I'm okay with sending the report."

I wasn't copied on the note that was sent, but two hours later, I was copied on the response from the construction manager on the project. The email was a scathing reply. It contained numerous comments: "I wasn't in touch with reality; I wasn't a team player, etc." I still have a copy of the e-mail somewhere in one of my files.

The business manager called me and asked me to come to his office. "We'll call the construction manager and talk about the report." I arrived at his office a few minutes later, and he said, "Please close the door." He proceeded to call the construction manager, and for approximately the next ninety minutes, we sat and listened to him rant. His last comment, "With this kind of negative help, we don't want you to come back."

After the call ended, the business manager said, "I know you are scheduled to go back to the slope tomorrow, but if you are uncomfortable with what has happened, I understand. And you have plenty of work to do here."

I half-laughed. "You guys are paying me to help. They need the help, so I will go up and do what you are paying me to do."

He gave a simple response, "Okay."

I left his office, perplexed by the events, but knew that I was doing the right thing, trying to help. I really wasn't looking forward to returning to a hostile environment, but sometimes, in projects, it is a pressure cooker. There are a lot of people, under immense stress, and sometimes, the emotions take over.

The following day, as scheduled, I traveled to Alpine. Little did I know, but the construction manager was waiting for me to arrive. I had barely stepped into the building when he approached and directed me to his office. I followed him to his office, wondering what was coming. It was more of the same tirade from yesterday. One of the last comments he made has stuck with me for many years, and I still laugh about it. "Why don't you stand in the dish room, with a clipboard, and ask every MF'er that brings in F'ing dirty dishes, when they think we're going to start up!?"

I tried to smooth ruffled feathers. "I'm here to help, not to hinder. Let me work to build a database to track work, build a schedule, and we'll get the team around the table to make sure everyone is on the same page." I don't remember exactly what he said, but basically I had a week to put something together. I worked 18-20 hours per day the next four days, employing the help of several others.

At the end of the week, I had all the information, the schedule, and the supporting documentation. I printed copies for the meeting attendees. We reviewed everything, page by page. At the end of the meeting, the team agreed with the information and determined that we would start up by October 31, plus or minus two weeks. We were off by a day. Alpine went into production on November 15, 2000.

I remained friends with the construction manager and worked several projects with him and the team. There was never any ill will. It's a job, and sometimes the stress of the job takes over.

CHAPTER TWENTY-FOUR

THE BAG DRAG

Anyone who has used airlines to travel probably has a story of lost luggage. This is a story of a lost backpack…

We had just completed a major facility expansion at Alpine, along with the construction of facilities on two new drill sites. I was being transferred from Alpine to Kuparuk, in a similar role as a construction supervisor. I was excited for the opportunity to work at Kuparuk on new projects. I worked the first part of my two-week hitch at Alpine, and then I would fly to Kuparuk for the remaining week of my hitch.

I was a little sad to be leaving Alpine. I had been there several years and had worked alongside a lot of good people. Alpine was still relatively new and small, like a family. Normally, without any construction going on there are approximately 250 people on shift.

I packed up all my worldly possessions from my office and my room in the camp. I had a duffle bag full of cold-weather and fire-retardant clothing, and another duffle bag full of clothes and toiletries. I took those two bags to security, where they would be transported to Kuparuk on one of the small aircraft that flew back and forth between the two fields.

"Good Morning, John," the security officer said.

"Morning, I'd like to send these two bags to Kuparuk. Today is my last day here at Alpine," I responded.

He instructed me to take the bags to the luggage rack, and he would be down momentarily to weigh them and tag them. I did as instructed and waited in the baggage rack area.

The security guard walked into the baggage rack area. "Man, I hate to see you go. You're one of the good guys in projects. You're like a fixture around here."

I laughed. "I will definitely miss all the great people I have worked with here over the years. Y'all have become my second family."

He individually weighed each bag, tagged them, wrote the flight number on the tag, and handed me the stub from each tag.

"I'll probably have another bag and a box a little later. I'm still packing things," I said.

"No problem. When you get them packed, bring them down."

I went back to my room in the camp and packed up the remainder of small items. I had a nice oversized laptop backpack that was the perfect size for the remaining items. I did one last look through the drawers and closet to make sure I had everything. I took one last look around the room and let out a heavy sigh. This was the last time I would see this room.

I walked through the camp, stopping in the chow hall for coffee, and then went to my office. I found a small box to pack the things in my office that I wanted to take with me. I carefully placed the items in the box, arranging things so that I could get everything in a single box. It took several attempts to fit everything in one box, but eventually I made the jig saw puzzle fit together.

I taped the box shut and then taped a label to the outside. I thought, "I better take these to security and get them on the plane." Sometimes, there was too much to carry on the plane, so things that were checked in early had a better chance of being at Kuparuk when you arrived.

I walked into the security office. "Hey, Jon. I have the rest of my junk ready to ship to Kuparuk."

He laughed. "I'm sure it's not junk. I'll meet you in the baggage rack area."

I carried the items down the hall, thinking about my departure. Jon was right behind me, and, just like before, he weighed each item, tagged it, wrote the flight number on the tag, and handed me the stub. "There ya' go, will you have anything else?"

I shook my head no. "That's it, other than my briefcase, which I will carry with me."

Later that day, I departed Alpine for the last time. The flight from Alpine to Kuparuk is about fifteen minutes of actual air time. As we landed, I thought, "Welcome to your new home." As I climbed down the stairs of the plane, I realized that I might not be on that little plane for a long time, maybe never again.

I checked in at security, received my room assignment, and walked the long hallway down to my new office in "O-Wing." It was the farthest office wing from the main camp and where the projects/construction guys were officed. I met the other team members, many of whom I had talked to on the phone but never met in person. My new alternate took me to our office. We would share the office for a week before starting our rotation.

"I'm probably going to leave early to go unpack my

stuff in the room in camp. Unless there is something pressing that you need me to stay for?" I asked.

He shook his head no, "Nope. Go ahead and get settled into the room." Even though I wouldn't be sleeping in the room, I wanted to unpack some of my stuff in the permanent room.

I made the long walk back to the camp wings, stopping at the luggage area to grab my stuff. Three of the four items that I shipped were sitting on the rack. I grabbed the two duffle bags and hauled them upstairs to the camp. I unpacked what I wouldn't immediately need for the next week in my room. The other bag I dragged to my temporary room.

I left the box with the stuff from the office sitting on the baggage rack and figured I would just grab it in the morning when I walked to the office. After unpacking, I decided it was dinner time, so I headed to the chow hall. It was Wednesday, that meant steak for dinner. The line was long to get dinner, but it usually moved quickly. After dinner, I was feeling a little tired, so I headed to my room. I realized about halfway there that my alarm clock had been packed in the backpack. The backpack was the missing item from earlier. I did an about face and headed for the luggage area.

When I arrived in the room where the luggage was racked, I looked around. All the shelves were empty. No backpack. This wasn't good. I headed upstairs to the security desk. "Hi, Larry. I just transferred over from Alpine today, and one of my bags is missing," I stated, reading his name from the tag on his uniform.

"What's your name, sir? And do you have the tag stub?" he asked.

I pulled the stubs out of my wallet and slid the one for the backpack across the counter. He picked up the phone and called security at Alpine. "Hey. This is Larry at Kuparuk. We're looking for a backpack. The tag number is...okay, I'll hold." He looked at me. "They're going to look and see if it is still on the rack at Alpine."

Larry and I chatted while we waited for them to go look. After about ten minutes, Larry started talking to the individual on the other end of the line, "Okay. Thanks for looking. Have a good night. I'll send a note to SSA (Share Services Aviation)."

He replaced the receiver in the cradle, "Well, the bag isn't at Alpine, but I'll send a note to SSA to see if it showed up in Anchorage." I wondered how the bag could be in Anchorage, but sometimes strange things happen when flying. "Check back tomorrow after lunch," he said.

I nodded. "Okay thanks for your help."

I headed off to my room to get some rest, wondering, hoping, that I would wake up without the assistance of an alarm clock. Needless to say, I did not sleep well, worried about oversleeping and in a new bed and new surroundings. The following morning, I woke with at start at 3:45 a.m. I figured I would hit the gym since I was awake, and I normally got up around 4:00 a.m. anyway.

I worked out, showered, had breakfast, and went to the office around 5:30 a.m. The morning flew by. There was much to learn and understand on the first day. My new alternate was inundating me with information. It was like drinking from a fire hose. At 11:00, he said, "It's lunch time. Let's go eat."

As we walked by the security desk towards the chow hall, I said, "I'm going to check on my bag. I'll catch-up with you in the chow hall." He proceeded to the chow hall.

"Good morning. I'm John. I'm wondering if you guys have heard anything from SSA on my lost bag?"

Hugh was on duty. "No bag, but they sent the form for

you to fill out for a lost bag." He slid a form across the counter. "Fill this out and send it to the e-mail address on the form."

I took the form and thanked him. My curiosity got the best of me. "Do we lose a lot of bags?"

He laughed. "No, not very often, but it does happen. I'm sure it will turn up."

After lunch, I filled out the form for my lost backpack and submitted per the instructions provided. I didn't expect the process to move quickly but received an e-mail response by the end of the day. The claim was being reviewed and processed, and I would be reimbursed for the bag and its contents by the end of the week. "Cool," I thought.

Several days passed, and I was walking by the security desk on my way to the office when Larry stopped me. "Hey, John. I have some good news for you. I got a phone call from SSA in Anchorage; they located your lost backpack and are shipping it up on one of today's flights."

I laughed. "Thanks. Where did they find it? Had it fallen out of the plane on the way over from Alpine?"

He laughed along with me at my attempt at humor. "No. It was found under one of the luggage carts in Anchorage."

I was glad that they had found my bag, and it was on its way to me. At the end of the day, I checked in with Larry to see if the bag had arrived. I dialed the number for security.

"Security, this is Larry," said the voice on the other end.

"Hey, Larry. It's John. I'm wondering if my bag showed up?"

Immediately I hear, "Oh shoot. I forgot to call you. Yeah, it's here. I don't think you're gonna be happy. It's a little damaged." I thanked him and told him I'd stop by on my way to dinner.

As I approached, Larry was seated behind the security desk. He looked up, smiled, and retrieved the backpack from under his desk. He walked over to the counter and placed the backpack on the counter. "She's a little rough," he said.

I started laughing. "A little rough? It looks like it was drug across the tarmac."

After careful inspection of the bag, which was nylon, it looked like someone had taken a torch to the bag. It was partially "melted" on one corner. When I started to unpack it, the first item out was the alarm clock, and one corner was completely ground off. I asked Larry, "How many laps did this make around the airport?"

Laughing, he responded, "I'm not sure, but I do know that it was under one of those luggage carts that carries the luggage between the airplane and the terminal."

"I guess we have a new definition for bag drag..."

"Bag drag" is the term given to the action of "dragging" your luggage to security on the day you rotate off-shift.

The follow-on to this story:

Larry and I remained friends through my years of rotating and traveling to the North Slope. Every time Larry was working baggage detail for the flights, I would joke about having someone else take care of my bags, or Larry would make jokes about no one else touching my bags, that only he knew how to take care of them.

CHAPTER TWENTY-FIVE

THE 2 GALLON WATER HEATER

I woke up a normal time, 4:30 a.m., and started my daily routine. I turned on the shower, brushed my teeth, and then entered the shower. When the ice cold water hit my skin, I was instantly awake and jumped back out of the shower. "What the hell?" I thought to myself. I checked the faucet to make sure the hot water was still on. Yep. I then tried the sink. No hot water there either.

I couldn't go to work without a shower, so I managed to endure the fastest cold shower I could take. I guessed that I missed my opportunity for a hot shower by sleeping until 4:30 a.m. I made the determination that tomorrow I would set the alarm for 4:00 a.m. and should be able to get a hot shower.

The following day, the alarm sounded at 4:00 a.m. I was up and out of bed quickly. I repeated my daily routine. I went into the bathroom, I turned on the shower, stood at the sink, and brushed my teeth. This time, rather than jumping right into the shower, I stuck my arm in the stream of water coming out of the showerhead. "What the hell?" The water was again ice cold. Again, I took a quick, ice cold shower.

Later that day, I called the camp manager's office. The phone rang several times, and voicemail finally answered. I waited for the beep. "Hey, Tom. This is John. I have a problem in the rig camp.Call me back at your convenience." After hanging up, I walked down the hallway to the dining room for a cup of coffee, and Tom was sitting there at one of the tables with several of his employees.

I walked through the food service area, made myself a cup of coffee, and then walked over to the table where he was seated. "Hey, Tom. I just left you a message. Have you got a minute?"

He nodded yes. "What's going on?" I explained in detail about the cold shower and lack of hot water. After I finished, he stated, "I'll go take a look at it to see if I can figure out what's going on." I thanked him and returned to my office.

Shortly after 3:00 p.m., the phone started ringing. I didn't recognize the number but answered anyway. "Hey, John. It's Tom. I think I figured out the hot water issue. Can you meet me in your room in camp?"

I checked my calendar to make sure I didn't have an upcoming meeting. "Sure, give me about ten minutes to get there. See you in a few."

I walked over to the rig camp, and Tom was waiting outside my room. "So, what's the deal with the hot water?" I asked.

He started laughing. "There's nothing wrong with the hot water. It works fine. I think there is a supply problem though." I was a little perplexed. "Go ahead, open the cabinet under the sink."

I gave him funny look, and said, "Okay." When I opened the cabinet doors under the sink in the bathroom, there was a 2-gallon hot water heater. "That's the hot water supply for your room." He started laughing.

During the construction of Alpine, because there was not enough room to house everyone, several portable camps were brought in to provide additional so bed space. I was fortunate enough to have been assigned to one of the rig camps. Rig camps are designed to be portable so they can travel with a drilling rig. They are self-contained. I was assigned the Company Man's room. It was the only single status room. It not only had space for sleeping but an office, and it was the only room with a private bathroom.

I learned to take a navy shower…

CHAPTER TWENTY-SIX

I FOUND $1.33

There are many different perspectives in the world. Perspective is based on knowledge and experience. Rarely will two people have the exact same perspective on something.

I was sitting at my desk, reviewing reports for the upcoming meetings in the afternoon when one of my peers walked into my office. "I finally figured it out, where the contractor's report was wrong," she stated proudly.

I had no clue what she was talking about, so I asked, "What are you talking about?"

"Well, there was a discrepancy between the contractor's report and what we had actually been billed for. I finally figured out the discrepancy."

Now I was curious. "How big was the discrepancy?" She proudly flipped through several pages of the report and stopped on a page with a large red circle on it. "Right here. They are off by $1.33."

I shook my head and asked, "How long did it take you to figure this out?" I was being a bit sarcastic.

"I've been working on it all week."

I could tell she was proud of herself, and I didn't want to burst her bubble. "Good job, but in the future, before you undertake an exercise like this, please consult me."

In the grand scheme of things, she had just spent approximately $4,000 dollars of time to find $1.33. We were spending several hundred thousand dollars a day at the time, and the error wasn't going to bust the budget.

From her perspective, because she has a degree in accounting, that $1.33 was very important. But in an industry that spends millions every day, although it might be important, it was not at that particular moment in time. Getting oil production on-line was much more important.

CHAPTER TWENTY-SEVEN

THAT'S MY BOSS, THAT'S MY DAD

It was a typical Saturday night. I had gone to dinner with several buddies that I ride motorcycles with, and then we went to one of the local bars in Anchorage, Alaska: Chilkoot Charlies. The place is world famous, or so they advertise. It was a great place to go people watch, one of my favorite pastimes.

The place was usually busy on Saturday nights, but not on this particular weekend. As we stood there, talking and making fun of the folks in the bar, a rather attractive young brunette walked by and waved. I didn't recognize her but waved in return.

About twenty minutes later, we were getting ready to leave when she walked up. "Are you guys leaving already? It's only midnight."

I nodded. "Yeah, not much going on tonight. I'm just not feeling it." She reminded us that there was a concert going, the reason for there being few people here.

"I guess I'll see you guys next weekend. You guys are always here," she said.

"You may see these guys, but I won't be here. I have to go back to work," I informed her.

She laughed and stated again, "You guys are like a fixture on this corner. You guys are always here."

I shook my head. "Not me. I'm out of town half the month for work."

"Oh, do you work on the Slope?" she asked.

"Yup, I work in construction," I said.

She smiled. "Do you know a guy named…"

I was surprised to hear the name. "Yeah, he's my boss."

She laughed. "That's my dad. Don't tell him you saw me here."

I was surprised. "You don't have to worry about that. He and I don't have that kind of relationship. Strictly work related."

"Oh good," she responded. I wondered why anyone would be worried about being sighted at a bar, but it was none of my business. She then followed with another question, "What do you think of my dad?"

I was at a loss for words. This was similar to the question, "Do these pants make my butt look big?" There is no answer that doesn't get you in trouble.

I thought for a second, "He has his moments when he can be a stick in the mud." I breathed a sigh of relief, thinking I had dodged a real messy situation.

The look on her face said it all. "No. My dad is an asshole."

CHAPTER TWENTY-EIGHT

NORTH SLOPE FLIGHTSEEING TOUR

If you have never been to Alaska, pictures and words can do little justice to describe the beauty and vast wilderness. Alaska has everything from volcanoes and rainforest to frozen tundra. Most of the state is not accessible by road. Therefore, "flightseeing tours" are one way to be able to experience the beauty.

I had the opportunity to see the North Slope, where most of Alaska's oil industry is, from the window of an airplane...

I was working for ConocoPhillips on the North Slope. I was assigned to Kuparuk but often flew to Alpine to offer support on projects there as well. On one particular trip, I was leaving Alpine for the day and headed back to Kuparuk.

The bus used to transport passengers to and from the runway tarmac sat idling awaiting the arrival of the twin-engine Otter from Kuparuk. I was the only passenger on the plane, so the security officer/bus driver and I made small talk while waiting. "When are you going to go come back here permanently?" he asked.

I shrugged my shoulders. “I don’t know. Maybe when the next big project happens here. Right now, there isn’t much going on here. I go where they tell me.”

As we continued to converse, the plane approached from the east, circled around the Alpine facility, and started its descent to the gravel airstrip. We watched the plane taxi into the tarmac area, where passengers and their luggage would deplane. The plane came to a full stop, and we waited for the engines to power down. Once the props stopped turning, the pilot and co-pilot exited the aircraft.

The side door was opened, and the arriving passengers began to exit the plane from the rear. They were guided around the wing to the front of the aircraft where carry-on bags had been stored in the nosecone. Once everyone had exited the plane, I was allowed off the bus.

I carried my bag to the front of the plane and handed it to the pilot. “Evening, Walt.”

He responded in kind, and then stood there waiting for others to get off the bus. When he realized I was the only passenger, he asked, “Are you in a hurry to get back to Kuparuk?”

I laughed. “Nah, I’m done for the day. Just going to grab dinner.”

“Oh, how’d you like to go for a tour? We have to fly the rivers for break-up. It will take about two hours. Or we can just drop you at Kuparuk and then do it.”

I was not in a hurry and thought it would be interesting to see parts of the North Slope that not many get to see. “I’m game. Let’s go.”

During break-up in the spring, the plane was used to visually look at ongoing ice melting along the rivers. They visually looked at water flows, potential ice dams, ice flows, etc. It also allowed for trying to calculate when the bridge across the Kuparuk River would be impassable due to thawing conditions.

Since I was the only passenger on the plane, I had fifteen seats to chose from. I chose the very back row. This would allow me the best view from either side of the plane. Once the bus departed the tarmac with the arrival passengers, Walt and the co-pilot climbed into their seats in the cockpit. They worked through their pre-flight checks and then began their startup process.

Both engines running, we started our taxi out to the airstrip. We travelled the length of the runway, made a u-turn, and sat there waiting for approval to take off. Once we were given approval, the engines were throttled-up and the brake released. We sped down the airstrip and were airborne in seconds. We banked hard to the north, out over the Arctic Ocean momentarily. I assumed we were flying the Colville River but was not sure.

We flew for nearly two hours straight. Because of my unfamiliarity and the lack of discernable landmarks, I couldn't tell you everywhere we flew. It was an incredible flight. We circled high overhead over the largest gathering of caribou that I had ever seen, not once, but twice. I am sure there were tens of thousands of those resilient beasts that survived in the Arctic. I only wish that I had had a camera.

We followed one of the rivers; I assumed it was the Kuparuk river. We would bank left, bank right, and follow the winding path of the river. It was the most incredible flight that I had ever been on in my entire life.

As the pilots completed their mission to fly the rivers, I started to see familiar sites, the orange well houses and modules on Kuparuk drill sites. We must be getting ready to land. We slowly descended and eventually touched down on the gravel airstrip at Kuparuk. The engines were powered down, and we made the short journey down the runway to the tarmac. As we made the turn onto the tarmac, there was a bus waiting to pick up the only passenger, me. Walt turned around and looked at me.

"I'm really sorry. I forgot you were back there. I hope you didn't get sick."

The smile on my face probably didn't portray the thankfulness I had. I stated, "Sick!? Are you kidding? I had my own private plane, and I got to see parts of the North Slope that very few will ever see. That was the most fun airplane ride that I have ever had. Can we go again?"

Walt laughed…

CHAPTER TWENTY-NINE

GETTING PAID 23.5 HOURS A DAY

It is not very often that you work a job that pays you for almost every hour of the day, but sometimes it happens...

We were building two new drill sites in the Alpine field, on the North Slope of Alaska. One of the drill sites, CD3, is a roadless drillsite. There is no permanent road that connects the drill site to the central facilities. An ice road is constructed every year to support drilling operations, maintenance activities, and any construction projects.

The original plan for startup and commissioning of the drill site was to be in full production by the end of the ice road season, which is typically between April 15th and May 1st. Unfortunately, due to a myriad of factors, construction efforts were unsuccessful at achieving the target.

When the reality set in that the startup date was unachievable, planning was set in motion to complete the project in the summer, after the ice road had melted. Two helicopters were rented, along with the support of two fixed wing aircraft: a Boeing twin-engine Otter and a Casa 212.

The plan would be to work twelve hour shifts and do

changeout using the aircraft, primarily the fixed wing aircraft. The overall required manpower would be split equally to maximize efficiency of the aircraft. Approximately 100-120 personnel would be required to complete the work, 50-60 per shift.

Both aircraft would comfortably seat fifteen passengers, so there would be four flights starting at 6:00 a.m. each day. The round trip was approximately thirty minutes by the time you loaded passengers, made the flight, offloaded, and then reloaded. Personnel were assigned flights based on their crew, and efforts were made to ensure that full crews arrived and departed at the same time.

The process worked as efficiently as possible until one day… The weather on the Arctic coast usually brings fog. Sometimes that fog could last for days. The longest I experienced was about ten days. When the fog rolled in, aircraft were unable to fly due to the lack of required instrumentation systems on the ground.

We had planned for some adverse weather and what to do if the crews got stranded at the work location. We had purchased sleeping bags, emergency water and food, and a large industrial tent to serve as "the camp." The one thing that had not been discussed was the question, "Will the personnel be paid for their time being stranded?"

It was a great question, but there was no clear answer because no one on the staff had faced a similar situation in their careers. Both the legal and human resources department were consulted on the issue. After several meetings and lengthy discussions, it was determined the interpretation of the labor law was that guys would be paid for every hour, less the normal thirty-minute lunch period. Therefore, if a person was stranded overnight, they would be paid 23.5 hours per day.

The craft personnel loved the fact that they would be paid 8 hours of straight time, and an additional 15.5 hours of overtime if they were stranded. Additionally, North Slope policy was that Saturday and Sunday were automatically overtime days. Many guys complained about the accommodations if they were stranded but celebrated how much money they were making.

We had one individual think that he could buck the system. He intentionally hid in the bathroom and missed his flight back to the main camp, thinking, "I'm gonna make some extra money for getting stranded."

Unfortunately, what the individual didn't count on was the fact that he had been given an opportunity to get on the plane, as scheduled. He made the choice to miss the flight. Therefore, because the company was not at fault for him being stranded overnight, he would not receive additional pay. His employer also made the decision, because he intentionally missed the flight, that he willfully tried to steal from the company. He was promptly terminated.

CHAPTER THIRTY

LOOK I'M EATING HEALTHY

One of the remarkable things about the oil industry is the broad diversity of the people that you work with. You don't usually get to pick and choose the team you want like in the schoolyard. Companies and employers try to put their best skilled people on teams where they think they would best fit.

I've met many interesting people during my three-decade career in oil and gas. Some are still friends, some were never friends, some were great mentors, and some have left us. This particular person was one of the most unique individuals that I ever met. We became friends, bonded through our physical size as big men, oversized men.

Jon was an extremely smart individual. He worked in our quality department. He was also a very old-school individual who refused to grow up, and he had a love for food like no one I had ever met. Jon was a huge man, probably six-foot-six and all of four hundred pounds. And he loved food.

One of the many stories regarding his love of food

involved popsicles. There were eleven of us sitting in a training class for Safety in Motion. We were fifteen minutes into the training session when Jon arrived. As he entered the classroom, he was eating a popsicle.

One of the women in the room made a comment, "Did you bring enough for the rest of us?"

Jon laughed. "Well, I'm not sure I brought enough," he said as he reached into his pockets on his Carhart overalls. He pulled out at least half a dozen popsicles, held them up and asked, "What flavor do you want?"

Jon was known around camp for his love of food. Wednesday dinner was steak night, and Jon would order up two or three steaks, and if there were crab legs, he wouldn't take a plate; he would just load up the tray with crab legs.

Well, one day, Jon disappeared. We later found out that he was rushed to the hospital on his day off for open heart surgery, quadruple bypass. It would be several months before he was released to return to work.

Eventually, Jon did return to work, and I was impressed to see him trying to make improvements in his lifestyle choices. I would see him in the gym, walking on the treadmill, skipping the ice cream machine for dessert, and generally making healthier food choices.

I was busy working in my office one morning when Jon walked by. He stuck his head in my office. "Morning. Look, I'm eating healthy." He held up two small bowls of fruit.

"Jon, I'm happy for you. You were given a second chance on life, and I'm glad that you are making the most of it."

A few hours later, he walked by my office, this time he was carrying a to-go box. I yelled out the door, "Hey, Jon." He stopped and came back to my office. "What's in the box,

Jon?" I asked. He tried to ignore the question. "What's in the box?" I asked again.

Reluctantly, he stated, "A couple pieces of bacon."

I shook my head. "Let me see."

He opened the lid to the box, there were probably two pounds of bacon in there. "Jon, come on. I know you love food, and who doesn't love bacon? But you're killing yourself."

CHAPTER THIRTY-ONE

MY ABILITY TO CALL BULLSH!T

Sometimes, some of us have little control over the words that exit our mouth. Our mouths work faster than our brains. We say words and phrases that, if given a second of thought, we would never utter. I was a slow learner. Even to this day, sometimes I will say something before I think it all the way through.

I had been invited by a former peer to rejoin a group in Alaska for executing projects. I had left the group two years before and was tired of being gone from home. I missed family and friends and had made the decision to come back home.

One of the standard business processes used to hire people was the use of an interview team. The team usually consisted of three or four individuals. Sometimes they interviewed as a team, sometimes individually. If the latter method was used, the interviewers would meet after the last person conducted their interview, and notes were compared.

I was offered a position and had submitted my resignation to my current employer when I received a phone call. "Hey, John. We just received notification that the ConocoPhillips team wants to interview you." I was being hired through a third party, so I thought this was a little odd but agreed to an interview. A date was set.

I arrived at the ConocoPhillips building in Anchorage, Alaska and checked in with security. "We'll call the individual. Please have a seat over there." I did as instructed. I sat patiently waiting for the hiring manager to arrive to escort me upstairs.

He was expecting me, and I was surprised that I was kept waiting for thirty minutes. He finally arrived downstairs. I stood and walked over, shook his hand, and said, "Thanks. Good to see you again." He took me to the security desk where my ID was checked, and I was given a "visitor's badge."

As we rode the elevator upstairs to the tenth floor, we made small talk about my work in Russia. "We're excited to have you back on the team. We have a lot of upcoming work, and we are glad to have you back on the team."

We stepped off the elevator onto the tenth floor. It hadn't changed since the last time I was in the building, several years before. He scanned his security badge, which activated the automatic door, and we stepped through the doorway. "Do you want coffee or water or need to use the restroom?" he asked.

I shook my head, "No thank you sir. I'm good."

We entered one of the conference rooms on the floor. Seated around the table were three other individuals, all guys that I had worked with previously. They were all mid-level managers in differing roles.

The next two hours were excruciating. I was grilled like an overcooked steak on a barbeque grill. I kept thinking, "Man, I've worked with all you guys before." When the questions finally stopped, I'm sure I was flushed. I needed to use the restroom, and I was wondering what the ulterior motive was for what I had just experienced. The four managers looked at each other and agreed that they did not have any more questions for me.

I thanked them for the time and the opportunity. I stood and was preparing to leave the conference room when the construction manager spoke up. "Wait, I have one more question. What do you think your biggest asset is that you bring to this team?" he asked.

I didn't give it one microsecond of thought. "My ability to call bullshit. If it looks like a duck, sounds like a duck, and walks like a duck, it's a duck."

I think my response surprised the construction manager. He had this look. One eyebrow would raise over his wire frame glasses. I got that look. I thought to myself, "Crap, I just lost the job. I better call the guys at Exxon and tell them that I needed my job back."

I did not lose the job and eventually progressed through my career to replace the construction manager. He appreciated my no-nonsense response.

CHAPTER THIRTY-TWO

BULL IN A CHINA SHOP

I worked in the field for several years before being transferred to the office in Anchorage, Alaska. I wasn't given a choice about the transfer, and I wasn't looking forward to not having a mini vacation every two weeks. I had been working a rotation schedule since entering the oil and gas business, and it was nice to have the time away from work.

The phone rang in my office. "Hey, John. I'm calling to let you know that this will be your last rotation on the Slope. We've made the decision to transfer you to town," the boss said. He continued, "Don't worry. We're not going to cut your pay. It will be a lateral move, but you won't get the additional bump for the remote site."

"I hope I haven't done anything wrong. I really enjoy working in the field," I stated. "No, you haven't done anything wrong. It's an opportunity to learn another part of the business," the voice on the other end of the phone said.

"I guess I don't have a say in the transfer?" I asked. After the phone call ended, I sat at my desk, disheartened.

The next several days, I packed all my gear and said goodbyes to all the great folks I had been working with. In my mind, I wanted to tell the bosses to kiss my butt, but I did not want to risk being unemployed, so I played along.

The plan was for me to take my normal two weeks off and then report for work the following week on Monday. The time off passed too quickly, and it was doomsday, time to report to the corporate office for my next job assignment. I even went shopping for corporate office attire, including a tie. The tie wasn't required, but I included it because I had always joked about not being able to work in the corporate office because I didn't own Dockers and Polo shirts.

I arrived promptly at 7:30 a.m. My boss had yet to arrive, so I had to sit in the lobby and wait for him. I did not possess a badge for the corporate office, so I was denied entry. Finally, around 8:00 a.m., the boss arrived. We exchanged niceties, and I was issued a temporary badge by building security.

He escorted me to my office, which looked like it was vacated in a hurry. There were stacks of paper everywhere and boxes full of who knew what. "Go ahead and get settled in. Come to my office at 9:30 a.m., and I will escort you to the badging office," he said while leaving me to fend for myself.

At 9:25 a.m. I started searching for his office. I knew the number but was unsure of exactly where it was located. I wandered the hallways, seeing the names on doors of people that I had never met in person but had interfaced with over the telephone. I eventually found his office, walking almost in a complete circle around the floor.

"I'm ready for my badge," I said.

He turned around from his computer. "Okay, let's go. I'm kind of busy, but we need to do this now. The badge lady is very strict about the hours, and if we show up late, you won't get a badge until this afternoon."

We exited the floor into the elevator lobby. He pushed the button to go down, and we waited for the arrival of a descending elevator. As we entered the elevator, he pushed the button for floor number two, where the badging office is located. "How are things going so far?" he asked.

I laughed. "Well, the first two hours of my day have flown by, and I've accomplished nothing other than cleaning out the cabinet so that I can hang-up my jacket. And I'm still wondering why I am here."

"After we get your badge, we will go to my office and talk," he stated.

The badge process was pretty simple: fill out a half-page form with basic information, get your picture taken, and wait for the badge to print. The boss waited in the hallway. Once I had my badge, I was given instructions on how to sign up for the building training and informed, "Failure to complete the building training will result in your badge being de-activated."

On a side note, I tried to remove the tie I had worn as a joke, but the boss would not let me remove it for the badge photo. I was the only guy in the construction organization wearing a tie in his photo. Lesson learned, do not wear a tie on picture day.

We returned to the floor where the boss' office was. I followed him to his office and sat down in the chair across the desk from him. "I want to answer your question from earlier. It is important for you to learn the whole business, not just the field execution piece. It will help your career. The other reason that you were transferred was to work on 'you.' Your "bull in a china shop" approach is going to kill your career."

I was perplexed by the statement and responded, "You

pay me to make things happen. That is what I do. I make things happen."

The boss laughed. "Yes, you do exactly what you are paid to do, but the carnage you leave behind is going to hurt your career. You have to learn to be able to be more gentle in making things happen."

To this day, it was some of the best career advice I ever received. I didn't think so at the time, but I listened. I tried to be more understanding, more willing to listen, more willing to consider all solutions rather than just the one that I wanted. Years later, the guy that gave me that opportunity and advice ended up working for me, so I thanked him for helping me be successful.

CHAPTER THIRTY-THREE

WHERE IS MY BALL CAP

Sometimes in our lives and in our careers, we meet people who influence us, teach us, mentor us, coach us, or just give us a funny experience to reflect on.

During the construction of the original Alpine Oilfield on the North Slope of Alaska, I had the opportunity to become acquainted with one of the vice presidents of Arco Alaska, Inc. Arco Alaska eventually became ConocoPhillips Alaska, after several mergers and acquisitions. The year was 2000.

Ryan and I were having dinner one evening in the chow hall at Alpine. We were discussing golf, and he mentioned that he was preparing to attend the U.S. Open golf tournament. "That's gong to be awesome. Some day I would like to attend a PGA major event," I said.

He laughed. "I'll bring you back a hat. I know it is not the same as attending, but…"

I was in awe that I was going to get a hat. Not just a hat, but a hat from a major golf tournament, and from the vice president of the company. That was the last time I saw Ryan in person, until 2012…

Ryan had recently taken over as the CEO of ConocoPhillips. He was visiting Alaska for the first time as the CEO of the company. As we entered the ballroom at the Marriot Hotel, located next to the Anchorage office, I saw Ryan standing at the back of the room. I noticed that he was alone, and everyone seemed to be avoiding him. I walked up, held out my hand. "Hey, Ryan. Congratulations on the new position." He thanked me and shook my hand.

"I have a couple of issues though," I stated. He looked perplexed. "You probably don't remember me from our days at Alpine, back in the Arco days, but you promised me something back then. I've been waiting for twelve years. We were having dinner one night at Alpine, and you promised me a ball cap from the U.S. Open." I looked at my watch. "I've been patiently waiting for all this time."

He chuckled. "You've got a mind like a steel trap."

I laughed. "Yeah. All kinds of stuff gets trapped in my mind, frequently."

He then asked, "What's your other issue?"

I thought for a second. "Well, you and I stayed in touch for a few years after you left Alaska. I always thought that you would return to Alaska to be the president for Alaska. You skipped all those steps and went straight to the top."

He laughed. "The funny thing is, back when I was here, every morning when I would pull into the parking garage, I would look at Kevin Myers' parking space and think to myself, 'one day I'm going to park there.'"

I laughed. "You can park anywhere you want. I don't think anyone will say anything."

CHAPTER THIRTY-FOUR

WE'RE HUMAN, WE MAKE MISTAKES

I had just entered the hallway in the Kuparuk Operations Center (KOC). Heading toward me was one of the senior managers for the company. We walked towards each other. As we got closer, I asked, "Hey, Bill. How's it going?"

He stated, kind of angrily, "Not good. We had another recordable. I'm on my way to the meeting for the line call. I don't want to hear that someone just made a mistake. That's an unacceptable answer." His voice had become a little louder with every word.

"We're human beings, we make mistakes. Hopefully the injury is minor," I offered.

"That's a BS argument. There is no reason for anyone to get hurt. It's just an excuse," he insisted.

I thought for a second, "Even if we replaced humans with robots, robots are prone to error. They are programmed by human beings." He glared at me and walked off in a huff.

The good thing in the oil and gas industry is we have adopted a culture where we understand human behavior. Humans operate in an imperfect world. Regardless of procedures and protocols, at some point, humans will fail. The goal is for 'soft failure.' The automotive industry leads in understanding soft failure and incorporating it into their products. They know every driver will eventually be involved in an accident. Things like seatbelts, airbags, crumple zones, and impact sensors are all things that allow drivers to fail softly. The risk of serious injury or death is reduced by these features.

CHAPTER THIRTY-FIVE

THE TOILET SEAT IS FROZEN

Many of the rules and laws that govern our society are written in the blood of others, whether it was injuries or fatalities. The oil and gas industry is no different. Things like CFR 1910 and 1926 (OSHA sections of the Code of Federal Regulations) exist because of past of events. One of the events that changed the oil and gas industry forever was the Texas City incident in which 15 people lost their lives and 180 were injured.

One of the major changes to the industry was the adaptation of rules regarding facility siting. In other words, rules about where people could be situated within a processing facility and the associated risk of that location. Several new concepts have been incorporated into the risk minimization structure. Two of those concepts are blast radius and jet fire.

The blast radius is the potential impact caused by the explosion of hydrocarbons in a processing facility. If you are miles away from an explosion, there is a potential for energy to knock you off your feet, so to speak. If you are within feet of the explosion, the effect may be catastrophic, life altering, or deadly.

Jet fire is the release of hydrocarbons in a stream. Think of it as a flame thrower.

One of the projects that I worked in my career was the upgrade of facilities to meet new siting requirements. Sometimes, the facilities were relocated to a safer location, and sometimes the facilities were upgraded to "resist" an explosion or jet fire.

The decision was made by the company to move the control room at a central processing facility to a different location. The existing control room was deep in the center of the facility and, therefore, high risk. Several options were considered, reviewed, and reconsidered; new ideas were proposed, old ones revisited, and, eventually, all the stakeholders agreed on "the best" option.

The planning process was started, engineers and designers were engaged, and the project was off to what would be a marathon to complete. The concept being developed and eventually implemented was to repurpose one of the existing buildings farther away from the central processing unit in the plant.

The building chosen was the office complex, a three-story structure that housed the staff required to support the operation of the facility, and additionally one of the maintenance shops for the facility. A proposal was made to deploy a temporary office structure, thus allowing the demolition to be completed prior to start of new construction. This plan was quickly stopped by the occupants of the building. "Do you know how disruptive it will be for people to move twice?" was just one of the many comments made to the project team.

The team returned to the drawing board to devise a new

plan. What the team proposed was ingenious: staged demolition and reconstruction. Think of it like remodeling your house and doing it in sections: start with the master suite, move everything out of that area of the house, perform the demolition, and then perform the renovations and upgrades. Don't forget, moving the wall require the room on the other side of the wall to be be in a state of disrepair too.

The first part of the demolition was well under way when a discovery was made. If we remodel the bathroom, all the bathrooms in the building will become inoperable. Uh oh. A simple solution was implemented. Deploy a temporary bathroom facility outside the main building. It would have typical water closet features and could be powered off the existing electrical infrastructure, thus providing heat and lights.

The temporary bathroom was deployed and was operable. No one was happy, but the project moved forward. There were a multitude of changes to the plans and designs. This office is not big enough, this room isn't as functional as it should, this door doesn't match the others, etc.

The overall project took longer than it should have due to discovery work. Much like any remodel project on your house, you never know what you will find when you start opening the walls. The one thing that was consistent throughout the entire project was the complaining about the temporary restroom. It was a topic of discussion, weekly. "When are the new restrooms going to be operational?"

I was on site visiting the project. I usually travelled to the field several times per month to visit the projects and interface with the teams. During one of my last visits prior to commissioning the new office complex / control room, I visited the breakroom to grab a cup of coffee. There were several of the facility folks seated around the breakroom table. I walked in the room and, as a pre-emptive attempt, said, "Before you even ask, the new bathrooms should be available for use before the end of the week."

One of the guys seated at the table started laughing. "Hey, it ain't us complaining about the toilet. It's them women."

I shook my head and jokingly stated, "Uh huh. You guys are all such prima donnas."

The response came quickly, "No we are serious. They complain 'cuz they gotta put on arctic gear to go pee, and then when they finally sit on the seat, it's ice cold."

I laughed. "Seriously? That's the complaint? The toilet seat is frozen? I can get fur covers or, better yet, an incinolet." (An incinolet is an electric powered "turd burner." A paper liner is placed in the bowl prior to use. Upon completion, a switch is activated, and the waste is burned right in the bowl. If you've never used one, it's quite the experience.)

CHAPTER THIRTY-SIX

YOUR MOM DOESN'T WORK HERE

Oilfield workers often stay in camps at remote locations. Those camps may be part one of the permanent structures at a facility or a temporary portable camp. Most camps are modular sections constructed in a fabrication yard and then shipped to the installation location. Large camps are often fabricated as a sealift module, barged to an offload destination, and then transported across land to final installation location.

Camp conditions vary based on location, age, maintenance, etc. Some camps have individual sleeping rooms with communal showers/restrooms, while others have individual suites. Older and rig camps typically house 2-4 people per sleeping room with communal showers/restrooms. Offshore platforms, similar to a naval ship, may have sleeping accommodation rooms that hold 6-10 personnel. As the industry has changed from predominately male to more balanced, so have housing accommodations.

There are several benefits of working in a remote location that provides housing. Those benefits include not having to cook and perform household chores. In some locations, the camp staff will even wash and fold laundry for a small fee. There is a reasonable expectation for the individual to keep their room tidy, so that housekeeping staff can vacuum, dust, and change sheets (normally occurs once per week).

On more than one occasion, the following scenario, or one very much like it, happened…

The phone on the desk rang, and the caller ID identified the caller as "Camp Mgr." I wondered why the camp manager was calling, so, out of curiosity, I answered, "This is John."

The voice on the other end hesitated momentarily while they finished a conversation with someone else. "Hey, John. It's Doug. Are you busy?"

I thought to myself, "If I was busy, I wouldn't have answered the phone." I responded, "Doug, I'm always busy but always have time for you."

He began laughing, "Uh huh, sure. I have an issue that I need your help with."

I had no idea what kind of issue the camp manager would have that required the help of a construction supervisor. "What can I help you with?"

Doug asked, "Well, can you meet me at room D108 in a few minutes?"

I quickly perused my schedule on the computer to make sure I was free. "Okay, I can meet you there in about ten minutes." He thanks me and hangs up.

I wandered down the hall, stopping at the restroom at the end of the hall, and then headed into the chow hall for a cup of coffee. I prepared my coffee and made the short walk to D-Wing. Doug was standing outside D108, waiting for me to arrive. As I approach, he held out his hand and we shook. "Thanks for meeting me. I figured you needed to see this. This room belongs to one of your contractor's employees."

My curiosity was piqued. I was wondering what I was going to see when he opens the door. He slid the key into the lock, jiggled it back and forth to unlock it, and then rotated the handle to open the door. As he pushed the door open, he stepped aside to allow me to see into the room. I never imagined the sight that I beheld. "The housekeeper was supposed to change out the linens today, but they couldn't even get to the bed. This is the second time we have had an issue with this individual. Last time we just left a nice little note on the bed, asking the individual to make sure the room was kept up to allow the housekeeper to do their job."

The room was unsightly. There were dirty socks, underwear, and clothes strewn across the floor, the desktop was buried in half eaten meals, and the trash can was overflowing with garbage. "Please give the housekeeping staff my apologies. I will address this with the team tomorrow at their safety meeting. I don't know about you, but I don't know how anyone could live like this." Doug thanked me and we parted ways. I was perplexed and irritated that someone thought this was "okay."

The following morning at 6:00 a.m., the safety meeting kicked off. A normal list of topics were discussed, and, as always, I was given opportunity to speak. "First and foremost, I want to thank you for all the work that was completed safely. Second, I want you to think about all the great people working here and how their job is just as important as yours. Additionally, they face work conditions that are different from yours, but they work just as hard to make us all successful. I had a complaint from the camp manager yesterday. He showed me a room that one of you sleeps in. I won't single you out, but I want to make sure expectations for staying in the camp are clear. The housekeepers work hard to make sure you have a clean camp. This includes trying to keep the camp clean, specifically the rooms you stay in. Please pick-up your room when you leave for the day, so that the housekeepers can do their job."

There was an ensuing discussion about keeping the room clean and what that meant. "No, you don't have to vacuum, dust, or change your sheets, but you do have to keep the room picked up. Do not leave your dirty laundry laying around, and do not leave food waste in your room. Your mom doesn't work here, so clean up after yourself." The room was silent, the irritation was easy to read on my face. One gentleman raised his hand. "Yes, do you have a question?"

He was a younger guy and hesitantly said, "Yes, sir. I understand the point you are making, but my mom does work here." The entire room busted out in laughter, as I did not realize his mom did work there.

CHAPTER THIRTY-SEVEN

GATOR IN THE POND, DUCK IN THE WATER

Parts of the Alpine Central Facility were fabricated on the Kenai Peninsula in Alaska. It was the first time sealift modules were constructed in Alaska. If I remember correctly, the largest module was approximately 2,500 tons. Although heavier modules have been constructed elsewhere, it was a first for Alaska. During the construction, I was early in my career and learning new things about the industry. One of those things is the humor that existed in the workplace…

The radio squawked, “Russ O., copy?” Silence for a few seconds, “Russ O., copy?” Russ was the general superintendent hired to oversee the coordination of fabrication in the yard. The person trying to reach Russ made several additional attempts.

After about ten minutes of “Russ O. copy?” someone on the other end chimed in, “Go for Russ,” the voice sounding a little irritated.

“Where are you?” followed by a moment of silence. “Russ, you there?” was repeated several times.

An exasperated voice (Russ), “I’m taking a shit.” The

silence was deadening. He was serious. A few minutes later, Russ exited one of the porta-potties located on site. You could tell by his stride that he was not happy.

The story doesn't end there. A plan was set in place to have a little fun with Russ. Every time Russ would exit the main office building, a call would go out over the radio, "Gator in the Pond." This was an indication that Russ was out in the yard somewhere and to keep an eye out for him. If he entered one of the porta-potties, an additional radio call would go out, "Duck in the Water." It was when that call went out that folks would start calling for Russ on the radio. The poor guy wasn't able to use the restroom in peace for several months. Someone finally broke down and told him the code.

CHAPTER THIRTY-EIGHT

PORTA-POTTY NAP ROOM

Sometimes, we experience things in life which cause us to scratch our head and wonder what someone was thinking. I had a problem employee that worked for me years ago. I tried my best to coach, mentor, and train the individual but eventually had to make the tough decision to terminate her employment.

I shared an office with my team of five. We occupied one half of a double-wide Atco trailer. The office area was open, so there was little privacy. One morning, I spent little time in the office due to meetings in the main office complex. I returned to the office just before lunch.

"Where's Molly?" I asked my team.

No one could answer the question. "She was here about an hour ago."

Another responded, "I think she took an early lunch." The other just shrugged his shoulders. I had a couple work tasks for her to complete by the end of the day and knew that the sooner she started, the more likely she would complete the tasks before the end of the workday.

I went about completing a few of my own assignments

prior to lunch. The time flew quickly, and I heard the job-site whistle blow, announcing lunch break. I asked my team if anyone wanted to go to lunch, but they all declined, so I was on my own. I left the office and drove to one of the local dive restaurants a few miles away. I enjoyed a bacon double cheeseburger, fries, and a shake, filling the once empty void of my stomach. I really did not want to return to work but returned anyway.

When I arrived back at the office, Molly's desk was still vacant. I asked my team, once again, "Has anyone seen Molly?" I received the same response as earlier. She hadn't been seen now for several hours. I decided to check the parking lot to see if her car was parked there. Her car was parked in its usual place, just outside the security fence, just outside our office.

I was a little irritated because I had had problems with her hanging out in the main office with one of the other administrative assistants. I called the main office. "Hey, Kate. It's John. Have you seen Molly?" I asked.

"No, sir. I haven't seen her since 9 o'clock break," she stated.

"Well, if you see her, tell her I am looking for her and need her in the office post haste. Thanks." And I hung up. Now I was perplexed, but there was nothing I could do until she returned to the office.

About thirty minutes later, one of the other women in the office exited the back door to use the restroom, which was a pair of porta-potties staged just outside the door. When she returned to the office fifteen minutes later, she came and sat at my desk. "I had to walk across to the main office to use the restroom...because I think I found Molly."

I didn't understand what she meant by the statement and thought she was trying to make a joke. "What do you mean?"

She said, "Come with me, and I'll show you."

I chuckled. "Okay, I'll bite. Let's go."

As we exited the office through the back door, she whispered to me, "Go listen outside the women's porta-potty." I knew for sure this was some kind of joke now. I played along. I walked over to the women's porta-potty and pretended to listen intently. After several seconds, I realized that I did not have to pretend. The sounds I heard were real. Someone was in the porta-potty and snoring!

"You've got to be kidding me," I thought to myself. I shook my head and knocked on the door. No answer. I knocked again. Still no answer. I open handed slapped the door several times.

I heard rustling and a sleepy voice, "I'll be right out." My blood pressure was soaring by now, and I'm sure my face was beet red. I had never had anyone sleeping on the job. When she exited the porta-potty, I just looked at her and shook my head.

The next couple of hours were difficult. I did not want to lose my cool, so I waited until the next morning. I asked Molly and the on-site HR representative to join me in the conference room. "I'm sorry. We have given you multiple opportunities to improve your performance, but I am going to have to terminate your employment. Sleeping on the job is completely unacceptable."

CHAPTER THIRTY-NINE

A.R.E.

We live in an interesting world of texting and IM'ing, and everything is TL, DR (too long, didn't read). In the world of oil and gas, we call them acronyms. The industry has become encumbered with acronyms. Many companies maintain an acronym guide or dictionary.This allows you to understand what somebody might be talking about. I say might because one acronym may have more than one meaning. For instance, I.F.C. might be Incident Free Culture or Issued For Construction.

My first position working directly in the industry was as a construction engineer. Other terms for similar responsibilities include: construction supervisor, on-site construction manager, and field construction representative. And I'm sure there are a few more. I attended a meeting with the leadership team at Pump Station 1 of the Trans-Alaska Pipeline. The meeting lasted approximately two hours.

After introductions were made, the meeting commenced, and from that point forward, I was lost as to what was being discussed. It was out of sheer ignorance.

There was a secret code being spoken, the code called acronyms. Upon completion of the meeting, I asked my boss if we could talk when we returned to our offices. Of course, he agreed.

I explained to him the last two hours were impossible for me to follow along. I was clueless as to what anyone was talking about. I asked about several terms (acronyms) when the light came on for him. He started laughing and pulled out a little booklet, handed it to me, and said, "This little feller will help you learn how to speak oil." The booklet was the acronym dictionary.

Ten years later in my career, the organization I was working for decided to update their S.O.P.s and S.O.G.s (standard operating procedures and standard operation guidelines). One of the tasks on my list of documents to develop was the acronym dictionary. I spent the next several months reading all of our procedures and guidelines, talking to teammates, and capturing all of the acronyms.

The completion of the acronym dictionary was a major milestone for me. The completed dictionary was fifty, yes fifty, pages, 8 1/2" X 11" paper. I was proud of my accomplishment and coined my own terminology to describe our operating environment, "We are an A.R.E." : Acronym Rich Environment.

CHAPTER FORTY

PROSTITUTKA

I am sure that you have probably already guessed what the title of this chapter means, or maybe you searched online for the definition, but before you jump to conclusions...

While I was working in the Russian Far East, the hotel where we stayed was about a mile from the shipyard where we were building the topsides for an offshore platform. When the weather was nice, walking back to the hotel for lunch was a great way to get some exercise and fresh air.

One of my co-workers and I made the decision to walk to the hotel on a beautiful sunny day. As we approached the hotel, we observed something interesting. We watched as about a dozen beautiful, young women exited the hotel and climbed into a waiting minivan. I turned to him, "Did I really just see that?"

He laughed. "Yup, there must be a model convention in the hotel, and we weren't invited." The women were all tall, slender, and very attractive.

Upon entering the hotel, we were greeted by Sergei. "Good day, sirs. How are you?"

My co-worker was the first to respond, "Good. Who were them girls?"

Sergei laughed. "Prostitutka."

I immediately asked, "Those were prostitutes?"

He nodded, "Da, da, da."

I thought, "Wow, I would have never guessed." Out of curiosity, I asked, "Skolka?" Which is a loose translation of "how much?"

Sergei thought briefly and held up two fingers in a peace sign. "Two girls." He held up one finger. "One hour." He held up six fingers. "Six hundred rubles."

I did quick math in my head. "Bring the whole van back," I said jokingly.

Sergei had his cellphone out of his suit pocket and was already dialing. I had to stop him and explain that I was only joking! Six hundred rubles at that time was about twenty dollars U.S.

CHAPTER FORTY-ONE

WE'RE BOTH EDUCATED MEN

I became friends with a member of a national motorcycle club when I was twenty-one. Unfortunately, he passed at the young age of seventy. We chose different paths in life but shared a common bond of motorcycles. What I did not know was that we both also chose careers in the construction industry. He became a highly skilled craftsman, and I went into management.

I was sitting at home one day when my phone rang. I did not recognize the number, especially since it was from out of state, so I let the call go to voicemail. When my phone chimed alerting me that I had new voicemail, I had to find out who had called. I was surprised when I listened to the message: "Hey, Bud. It's your old friend Jack. I'm calling because I'm looking for work, and I heard you were managing work on the North Slope. If you don't find me a job, I'm going to have to move in and sleep on your couch." I chuckled to myself. It had been several years since we had talked or seen each other.

I called him back. "Hey, Jack. It's been years. Where are you living these days, and what are you up to?" We talked for a while and updated one another about life and what was new. I found out in the conversation that he was an instrument fitter/technician and been recently laid off. I didn't hire craftsmen directly but gave him a few leads for companies that I knew were hiring.

He was hired by one of the companies that we did business with and ended up working on one of my projects. I was impressed by his skill and craftsmanship, and the other thing that impressed me more than any of his work was that he took a young apprentice under his wing and taught him a true skill, something that would help the young man secure a future.

Jack worked on several projects under my purview over the next several years. Occasionally, I would run into him on the job site, and he would always give me a hard time about my position. "Big John. You and I are both educated men. You went to Yale. I went to jail," he would say. "Jack, you know I didn't go to Yale, but your point is made."

CHAPTER FORTY-TWO

I SHOULD HAVE BEEN A WELDER

The oil and gas industry employs millions of people, not to mention the jobs created by the influx of income earned by those employed in the industry. Every skill is required to make the industry function in a reasonable, efficient process. If you can think of a skill, at one point, it has probably been employed by the industry.

My chosen career was engineering, but the oil industry chose construction management for me. From my entry into the industry, I saw a future in construction. The industry is always building something new or refurbishing something.

I have worked in some sort of supervision most of my adult life. I enjoy the challenge of supervising and managing people. We are all unique, we all bring something to the table, and we all have a different perspective of the world. Additionally, we all have different motivators and drivers.

A career in management is rewarding and fulfilling, but also stressful. A good manager is willing to listen and learn. A good manager also understands the impossibility of knowing everything, and, therefore, hires people that have the skills they do not possess. Furthermore, a good manager will, more importantly, be a good leader, not just a good manager.

I often describe the manager role as someone who leads people to success, someone who manages when necessary, someone who dictates when necessary. Knowing when to employ each of these necessary skillsets is what will make a manager successful.

A good manager will also understand their own personality and how they interact with individuals. Think of someone that you are required to interact with that is "difficult." Does it always seem to be a struggle to work with a particular individual? Does a discussion often breakdown into disagreement? Do you know why? Learning how you will respond to people is part of a concept called emotional intelligence. As a manager, I feel it is important to understand the concept. It will help you in dealing with those difficult relationships.

Another aspect of a good manager is learning to deal with stress. Managers will always be subjected to stress. It is part of the job, although never written in the job description, roles and responsibilities, or necessary job skills. I developed several different coping skills for the stress: silence, isolation, exercise, and humor.

Silence usually meant I was doing a detailed analysis of information to determine if a reaction was necessary and what reaction to deploy. Most times when angered, I would grow silent and go into isolation mode. Often, I would close my door, not answer my phone, not respond to e-mails. This would ensure no regrets later.

Exercise was another way to deal with stress. I do not mean going to the gym lifting tons of weight or running a marathon. A simple walk around the outside of the building or a walk down the street sufficed to clear my head of the stress.

My favorite method for dealing with stress was to deploy humor. I can and will always find the humor in most things. Many of those that work for me always wondered how I was able to be upbeat and smile all the time. Humor. Life is way too short to let the stress of life bring you down. Find the humor in everything. You do not have to share your laughter or humorousness publicly, but in your own mind, think of what is funny about the situation.

Maybe you have dealt with the situation more than once. Maybe it is a situation you thought you would never have to deal with. Maybe, in the grand scheme of life, it is just funny (even if only to you).

I only transferred once for the company. I moved from Alaska to Texas. One of my memorable gifts from my going-away party was directly related to my deployment of humor to deal with stress. I received a rather large bag of going away gifts, and there was one large box, a welding helmet.

My team often heard me when dealing with the stress of the job state, "I should have just become a welder. When the whistle blows at the end of the day, you flip up your hood, turn-off your machine, roll-up your leads, and go home for the day. You don't get called on the weekends, on vacation, on your days off."

CHAPTER FORTY-THREE

THE PINK HARD HAT

During the construction of three major capital projects on the North Slope of Alaska, specifically the Alpine Development, we were struggling to execute the projects. We were building two new drill sites and a major upgrade to the central processing plant. The contractor we hired was struggling due to a multitude of issues. Everything from engineering issues to safety issues plagued us.

Owner companies and contractors are not paying you to get injured or to have incidents. The work, yes it's important, but not worth putting yourselves or others at risk. We had struggled throughout the project to make this message clear. My memory is foggy as to the actual statistics, but we a large number of recordable injuries and several lost time incidents.

We had a multitude of discussions amongst the management team about how we could improve the overall execution. Nothing was "off the table" for discussion. There were discussions about safety incentives, completion bonuses, adding additional safety personal to "watch," and many other ideas. Unfortunately, we did not land on a solution that was palatable to the team. We continued business as usual.

The weekly safety meeting kicked off with the normal safety stats: injuries and incidents for the week, BBS observations, hours worked, hazard identification cards, etc. It was easy to see the lack of interest by the roughly one hundred people in attendance. This was one of the issues: the message of not having an incident did not appear to be getting through.

As was typical with contractor safety meetings, at the end of the meeting, the floor was opened to the owner. I had been seated at the back of the room, so I stood and walked towards the front of the room. It was not unusual for me to speak at the meeting. I consider myself a good public speaker and have a connection with most in the workforce.

"I want you to pay attention. We, everyone in this room, myself included, are failing. We aren't delivering on expectations, we are over budget, we are behind on schedule, and, the worst part, we are hurting people. This has to stop. I am open to any ideas or suggestions." I then stood and looked around the room. Some guys looked down as I tried to make eye contact. Some just stared off into space. I continued, "I want to issue a challenge. The challenge is to complete the next thirty days without an injury, not even a first aid. If you meet this challenge, what's the reward?"

Again, the room remained silent. I could tell there were some wheels turning. The silence was broken by a familiar voice, my boss. "How about you wear a pink hard hat if we go thirty days?"

I kind of chuckled a little bit. "And you'll wear a pink

tu-tu." This brought laughter around the room. "I will gladly wear a pink hard hat if we can go thirty days without an injury," I stated.

Someone else chimed in, "You'll have to wear it all day."

And then another, "From the time you leave your room in the morning until you return to your room in the evening."

And someone else added, "Even while you are in the chow hall for eating."

I was okay with all the stipulations. "I will do it! A pink hard hat all day, but pictures will not be allowed. Challenge accepted on both sides. Now go do safe work."

The meeting adjourned, and everyone headed to the work site. I headed to our administrative aide's office. As I walked through the door, she piped up, "I heard you might be looking for a pink hard hat."

"Yep. Please try and find me a pink hard hat. I know they make 'em, but I'm not sure who makes them."

Over the next thirty days, not only did the safety of the project improve, but so did the productivity rates. Safe work is productive work. When you carefully plan what you are going to do, you minimize the risk, you make sure you have all the tools, materials, and equipment so that you are not starting and stopping.

The transformation was incredible. I was proud to don the pink hard hat on day thirty-one. I wore it from the time I left my room at 4:00 a.m. until I returned to my room that evening at 8:00 p.m. Several tried to take pictures, but they were stopped. I know of one picture, but I am also pretty sure that it was somehow destroyed.

I learned a valuable lesson from this challenge: money is not the only motivator. Something as simple as this challenge, which made it fun, will motivate people. To this day, I am proud of wearing the pink hard hat, but I am more proud of the hard work, attention, and dedication of the people doing the work that made it happen.

CHAPTER FORTY-FOUR

THOSE GUYS HAVE BEEN IN PRISON!

Stan's Palace was the construction offices built during the original construction of the Alpine Central Facility on the North Slope of Alaska. The office complex was a series of ATCO trailers connected by a hallway down the center. It was elevated on piles since it extended off the gravel pad.

It was about 7:00 p.m., and I was sitting at my desk in Stan's Palace. Ryan, our field HSE specialist (health, safety and environment) walked into my office. "You better go down the hall. There's a couple of guys mother f'ing each other, and I think they are fixing to throw down."

I half laughed. "Did you step in and ask what's going on?"

He looked at me with a strange look. "I'm not getting in the middle of those guys. They're longhairs, and they've been in prison!"

I laughed. "Most of those guys have been in prison. They are construction workers! I'll go check it out."

I walked down the short hallway from my office to the main hallway where the three "longhairs" were huddled up. As I approached, I quickly realized they were just ribbing each other and there was no impending "throw-down" about to occur. They were doing what most construction guys do, "flipping each other shit."

The impending disaster was avoided, and I think Ryan learned a little more about construction folk. They do know how to laugh, cut up, and have fun.

CHAPTER FORTY-FIVE

HOW DO YOU KNOW THAT GUY?

The weather was sunny and warm, perfect for the 4th of July. The weather brought out a huge crowd to watch the parade as it snaked its way through downtown Anchorage, Alaska. There were floats; fire engines; horses; old military vehicles; a bagpipe group in their finest kilts; Miss, Miss Teen, and Mrs. Alaska all riding in classic convertible muscle cars; and, of course, a group of motorcycle enthusiasts! Everything necessary for a parade.

I was part of the motorcycle group. At the time, I had hair down to my shoulders and weighed close to 400 pounds at six-foot-two. I was a "menacing" looking guy. I had donned my lightweight biker apparel – jeans, boots, t-shirt, and a denim vest. I rode a green Harley, affectionately known as "DA HULK." "Hulk" was also my biker name.

Parades typically move at a slow pace, and in warm weather, it is hard on air-cooled Harleys. The group rode in a waterfall formation to help keep the bikes moving and provide a little airflow in an attempt to keep bikes from overheating. A waterfall formation is two columns with room down the middle. The two riders from the back row would ride to the front, pull to the side, and stop. Kind of like "leapfrog."

I was completing my turn at leapfrogging when I heard someone yelling at me from within the crowd. "John. Hey, John!" the voice yelled. There, standing on the corner where I had stopped, was one of my bosses, Craig.

"Hey, Craig. How's it going?"

The parade moved forward, and once again it was my turn to leapfrog forward. I never thought about the conversation with Craig again, until a few days later in the office.

I ran into Craig in the hallway. He had to share his story about the parade. After the parade moved on, and I was out of sight, Craig's wife asked, "How the hell do you know that guy?" Craig had to explain that I worked for him. We both got a good laugh out of the story.

I always find it interesting how we stereotype people based on looks and appearances. And, obviously, Craig's wife had stereotyped me and wondered how her husband could associate with someone that looked like a biker.

CHAPTER FORTY-SIX

HEAT TRACE AND INSTALLATION

The oil and gas industry employs a diverse group of people from every corner of the globe. Sometimes people find themselves in a unique situation, and, rather than ask questions, they fill in their own blanks. Personally, I would rather ask questions if I were unsure or did not understand something. This individual, whose background was in finance, was someone that refused to ask if they did not know.

She earned the nickname, "The Blonde Bomber." She had bleached blonde hair and an extreme orange tan, and it was rumored she was a showgirl in Las Vegas at one point in life. She earned the name because of her appearance and her ability to "blow up" a meeting with her lack of understanding and refusal to ask questions to gain understanding.

The daily completion and handover meeting kicked off late in the afternoon, as usual. The incomplete work list was reviewed for items that were completed and the addition of any new discovery items (items that had been missed from the list). Typically, about twenty people were in attendance: project managers, superintendents, project controls, and quality inspectors.

We were nearing completion of the project, and systems were being completed and handed off to operations for purging and pressure testing. Anyone familiar with normal construction in the oilfield understands that heat trace and insulation are usually some of the last activities completed. Sometimes, they are completed after facility startup.

The meeting was coming to a close when the "Blonde Bomber" decided to interject, "You are not even close to starting up. The heat trace and installation is only 20% complete. How can you start when the installation is not complete!?"

We all stared in disbelief at the outburst. Someone asked, "What are you talking about? The overall project is greater than 95% complete."

She rolled her eyes. "Your report says that HT&I is 20% complete. You cannot start up at 20%."

Several of us looked at each with looks of dismay. The operations manager said, "We don't need insulation to start up. The only insulation that is needed is for personnel protection, and that is complete."

Again, she rolled her eyes. "I don't care about the insulation. I'm talking about the installation. We are only 20% complete!" Everyone sensed the rise in anger, which was uncalled for.

She was asked, "Would you care to explain what you are talking about?"

She sighed heavily. "You are only 20% complete with installation. You cannot start up if the installation is incomplete!" she said, her voice becoming elevated.

It became evident that she did not have any idea what she was talking about. One of the categories of incomplete work was HT&I, heat trace & insulation. She did not understand the terminology and refused to accept it when someone tried to explain it.

To this day, one of my peers and I make fun of the lack of understanding and the unwillingness of people to admit when they lack knowledge. We joke about the good ol' days of heat trace and installation…

CHAPTER FORTY-SEVEN

THE FLAMINGO TOUR

Just like many workplaces, there is always someone willing to bring humor. It was the late 80s in the oil patch in Alaska...

Kuparuk – which is a large discovery west of Prudhoe Bay, Alaska – went into operation in the early 80s and continues to grow. There are three central processing facilities and a seawater treatment plant. The overall field covers hundreds of square miles and falls under a single manager for field operations.

The field manager was offsite, and one of the superintendents was stepped up to act as field manager in his absence. This was a prime time for pranksters to come out of the woodwork. Someone, who was never identified, decided to place pink plastic flamingos around the field.

The radio airwaves were filled with flamingo sightings around the field. This was a first. Flamingos are not one of the migratory birds that normally show up in the summer. Some folks were gullible enough to believe that flamingos were truly migrating to the North Slope. What the prankster failed to anticipate was two additional events that occurred that day.

The first event was the arrival of musk ox in the field. Although it occurred, it was rare. Again, the radio chatter began about sightings of musk ox in the field. Normally musk ox travel in small groups. The largest that I have ever seen is twelve at once.

The final event of the day, which was the icing on the cake, was the arrival of a group of environmentalists to tour the field. It was never verified, but we are sure they saw the flamingos.

The timing of the flamingos was perfect, although the prank doesn't stop there.

That evening in the chow hall for dinner, one of the entrées was Cornish game hens. As was standard practice, leftovers were pre-packaged at night and stored in the spike room. The spike room is where personnel make their own lunch and snacks for the day. There are many choices, including the pre-packaged meals made from the leftovers of the previous evening meal.

The prankster took the time to prepare stickers for the leftover game hens. They were labeled "flamingo."

CHAPTER FORTY-EIGHT

MOTHER NATURE AT WORK

It is a rare occurrence in life to really see mother nature at work. We see the destruction caused by natural events like earthquakes, tornadoes, hurricanes, flooding, and wildfires, but we do not experience the true balance of an ecosystem. This story is one of mother nature at work.

I was working a corrosion investigation project along the Trans-Alaska Pipeline. This investigation occurred on the Chandalar Shelf of the Brooks Range, located approximately 170 miles south of Prudhoe Bay, Alaska.

A corrosion investigation is the process of excavating sections of the buried 48-inch pipeline to inspect the pipe for signs of external corrosion. Approximately half of the 800-mile pipeline is buried.

It was a beautiful winter day. I left my office at Pump Station 4 to travel to the job site located approximately an hour away. Pump Station 4 sits in a beautiful valley at the base of the Brooks Range Mountains. The gravel road follows a meandering river flowing through the valley floor. Eventually, the road winds up Atigun Pass, the highest point of elevation on the Trans-Alaska Pipeline. The elevation of the pass is 4,739 feet.

There is normally a small herd of caribou that wander the valley floor. On a normal day, they just kind of wander about, but on this day, they were at a full run. I thought to myself, "They must have drunk coffee this morning."

Another half mile up the road, I figured out why they were running. There was a group of 10-12 wolves hunting. I pulled to the side of the road to watch the action. I watched as the wolves chased and eventually circled one of the caribou. "Wow, this is amazing. This is the stuff you see on Mutual of Omaha's Wild Kingdom!"

Eventually, the wolves took down the caribou. Seeing this, I thought about how cool it was and wished that I had a video camera to record this action. It was long before the days of cell phones. At this point, the show was over for me, and I continued my journey to the job site.

Several hours later, after visiting the job site, I started my venture back to Pump Station 4. As I descended the winding road down the north side of Atigun Pass, I thought about the wolves and wondered if they would still be there, chewing on their freshly killed caribou.

I was surprised when I arrived at the location where the caribou had been killed. The wolves were no longer present, but there were probably a hundred ravens picking at the carcass left by the wolves. I guess they were hungry too.

That evening at the chow hall, I shared my story of the wolf kill. People listened intently and made comments about how lucky I was to see something like that. I couldn't disagree.

The following day on my journey to the job site, I stopped to make a final observation of the kill. To my surprise, it was nearly impossible to tell that a caribou had been killed there the day before. There were probably some bones in the snow, but even the blood stains had been stripped away by ravens.

The experience was a once-in-a-lifetime event and showed the power and balance of mother nature at work.

CHAPTER FORTY-NINE

SPEED KILLS

The Dalton Highway or North Slope Haul Road was constructed in 1974 to support the operations and maintenance of the Trans-Alaska Pipeline. It parallels the pipeline for approximately 414 miles. Originally, it was all gravel, but over time, approximately 25% has been paved. It is ranked as one of the most dangerous roads in the world. The danger is caused by inclement weather, road conditions, and the terrain it traverses.

The highway begins just north of Fairbanks, Alaska and terminates in Deadhorse, Alaska. There is little private vehicle traffic on the road, even though it is public. There are only three small towns along the route – Coldfoot, Livengood, and Deadhorse – populations of approximately 10, 22, and 25, respectively. Fuel is available but is at a premium price, and there are no public emergency services along the route. The closest medical facilities are in Fairbanks and Deadhorse.

Once you descend Atigun Pass, 170 miles south of Deadhorse, the road begins to flatten drastically. Once you reach Pump Station 2, the area is flat. I was told that there is only sixty vertical feet of elevation difference between Pump Station 2 and Deadhorse.

Prior to the invention of GPS tracking for vehicles, Alyeska Pipeline Service Company decided too many oilfield workers were speeding on the Dalton Highway. There is no police force working the road to enforce speed limits, so a new policy was rolled out.

"Effective immediately, all employees and contractors traveling on the haul road shall stop at each pump station and check in with security personnel at the gate. This will ensure the safety of all drivers on the road." Of course, the exact wording was probably different; this was my best recollection. The policy was discussed at toolbox safety meetings every day. We all knew the real reason for the policy change. They were tracking speeds along the road.

The truth came out within a week of the new policy being rolled out. A report was issued citing travel time statistics between pump stations. What made it more interesting was that the only speeder caught the first week was our boss.

CHAPTER FIFTY

SPEED KILLS - SAFETY NAP

As noted in the previous chapter, Alyeska policy required Dalton Highway travelers to check in at each pump station along the route.

I was traveling from Pump Station 4, approximately 150 miles south of Deadhorse. I had stopped at Pump Station 3 and Pump Station 2, and was on the final leg of the journey to Pump Station 1. It was a beautiful sunny day, and the road was free of snow and ice.

I used a timer during my travels to ensure that I did not arrive too early at any of the checkpoints. I was taking in the beauty of the drive but was not really paying attention to my speed. I arrived in Deadhorse about fifteen minutes earlier than I should have. I did not want to get in trouble for my inattention to speed, so I decided to make a pit stop at the store in Deadhorse. The store sold pretty much everything and was also the site of the Deadhorse Post Office.

I perused the store, killing time before heading to Pump Station 1. I wandered aimlessly, looking at things I had no intention of buying: native arts and crafts, books, magazines, clothes, household items, toiletries, everything in the store. Unfortunately, I really had not paid attention to how much time I had been in the store. One of my coworkers entered the store and approached me. "Hey. Pump 1 security is calling for you on the radio," he stated.

I looked at my watch. "Oh, crap." I had been in the store for thirty minutes.

I immediately exited the store and entered my truck. I keyed the mic, "Pump 1 security, copy?"

The voice on the radio responded, "Go for Pump 1 security."

I stated, "This is John Schuelke, checking in."

The voice on the other end said, "Are you good? You're late for checkin."

I thought quickly, "Yeah, I'm good. I was getting tired and pulled over for a safety nap."

The voice responded, "Good. Glad you are okay. Thanks for the update. We will see you soon." I had averted being caught speeding.

CHAPTER FIFTY-ONE

FIRST FOREIGN ROTATION

I was nearing the end of my six weeks at work and looking forward to being in my own home, hanging out with friends, and sharing stories of my first adventure into the Russian Far East. I was asked to stay a little longer. This is fairly common working rotation schedules. More often, it happens with craft personnel and not management, unless there is something really important occurring.

"Dobre utro, Vanya," Vladimir greeted me as I walked into the office that morning.

"Good morning," I responded.

"You wait," he said as he walked off.

I thought to myself, "I wonder what he's up to this time." He and I did not have a great start to our working relationship, and it was always contentious dealing with him. I waited, and after about ten minutes, he returned, Marina, the head translator, in tow.

"Good morning, John. Always nice to see you. Vladimir would like to converse with you." She smiled.

"Okay."

They conversed back and forth for the next several

minutes. With an exasperated look on her face, she said, "He says that you are not allowed to go home and must stay longer." I laughed. "I have to go home. My temporary visa is expiring."

Vladimir sneered at me and spoke to Marina. Even though I could not understand what they were saying, his tone become angry, and his face reddened. "He says that you must stay, and he will personally take care of your visa."

I shook my head side to side and said, "Nyet. Please tell him that my permanent visa application has already been submitted, and we are waiting on a response for the approval."

Again, they conversed back and forth for a few minutes. His anger was apparent. He was yelling at poor Marina. Finally, he pounded his fist on the table and stormed off.

"John, I am very sorry that he is so difficult," she said to me, sadness in her tone. "It is not your fault. I do not let people like him bother me."

After she departed the office, I sat thinking about what had just occurred. I knew the penalty for being in country beyond the visa date could result in me being denied access again, and, worse yet, time in the gulag. I wasn't going to prison for breaking the law in a foreign country.

The following morning, the alarm sounded at 3:30 a.m. I wiped the sleep from eyes and jumped out of bed, excited that I was going home today. I showered, packed everything in my bags, and headed down the stairs to the lobby. The time was now 4:30 a.m., and I was expecting the driver to be waiting in the lobby with my translator.

I sat in the lobby, impatiently waiting. Finally, at 5:15 a.m., the front door of the hotel opened, and the driver and my translator walked in. Marina was very apologetic for being late. The driver had not fueled the van the previous evening and had to wait for the gas station to open. We quickly loaded my belongings into the van and started our five-hour journey to the airport. We had plenty of time; the flight did not leave Khabarovsk until noon.

We arrived at the airport around 10:45 a.m. The driver pulled up to the front doors, and Marina and I unloaded my bags and walked into the terminal. We approached the ticket counter, where no one seemed to be working. The airport was about the size a small municipal terminal. The terminal itself was probably about 20,000 square feet. There were no fancy jetways, and you had to walk across the tarmac to the plane and board via old rolling stairs.

We waited patiently for someone to come to the ticket counter. After we waited for about twenty minutes, a young woman dressed in airline clothing came out of the door behind the counter. Marina asked for my ticket and passport. She began conversing with the woman behind the counter and handed her my ticket and passport. They talked for several minutes.

Marina turned to me and said, "You have missed the flight."

I was shocked and thought she was joking. I laughed. "That is not funny."

She proceeded to tell me that the plane had already departed. I was perplexed. "The flight is not scheduled to depart until noon. The departure time is right there on the ticket." She looked at the ticket and confirmed the departure time. Again, she talked to the woman behind the counter.

"The pilot decided to leave early," Marina stated.

"Okay, when is the next flight?" I asked.

The ticketing agent and Marina conversed again while

the agent was typing on the computer. "The next flight is tomorrow morning."

I was now frustrated. "I have to leave the country today. My visa expires today. What are we going to do?" Again, thoughts of going to the gulag flashed through my head.

Marina and the ticket agent conversed for a while, and then the ticket agent disappeared back through the door where she had appeared. "She is going to talk to the airport manager." We waited patiently at the counter, and the ticket agent finally reappeared thirty minutes later.

Marina and the agent conversed once again. "We have to go talk with the airport manager," Marina said.

We were escorted behind the counter and back into the office space. We were greeted by a portly gentleman who was the airport manager. "Hello, my friend. I am sorry to hear you have missed your flight," he said.

I wanted to say "I didn't miss the flight.; it left early" but did not want to argue. "How are we going to fix this?" I asked.

"We will send you tomorrow. I will make sure you have new connections," he stated. "What about my visa? It expires today."

He laughed. "Sir, that does not concern me. Only your flight."

I thought to myself, "Yeah, you don't care if I go to the gulag."

He smiled. "Sir, you will not get in trouble today unless you cause problems for the police. You will leave tomorrow. Okay?"

"Okay. What time tomorrow?" I asked. He began typing on the computer, and after a couple of minutes said, "I will fly you tomorrow in the morning, at 5:00 a.m."

I thought briefly and discussed driving back to Komsomolsk with Marina. "That's a long drive. If we return today, that means we would have to leave at midnight to drive back here. I think they should put us in a hotel for the night."

The manager understood what I was saying and started to speak in Russian. Marina and the manager argued back and forth in Russian for several minutes. I wasn't sure what was being said, but finally the manager stated, "Fine" and then glared at me. He picked up the phone and made a call. Again, the conversation reverted to Russian, and after several minutes on the phone, he hung up.

"You will be pleased; we have a room for you at the hotel. Have a nice day," he said. Marina and I left the office, collected my luggage, and exited the airport terminal. Sergei, the driver, was patiently waiting at the curb, smoking a cigarette. He snuffed out the cigarette when he saw us and walked over to help load the luggage into the van while he and Marina spoke.

Once the luggage was loaded, we drove through the airport parking lot and into the city. Marina explained to Sergei where we were going and asked, "Would you like to get something to eat?" I was starving. The last food I had was at dinner the evening before, and it was now nearly eighteen hours later. "What would you like to eat?" she asked.

"How about something like McDonalds?" I jokingly said, thinking that there were no McDonalds in Russia.

Marina apologized, "Our McDonalds closed. It only stayed open for a few months." I was surprised that there was a McDonalds in the first place but was wondering why it didn't stay open long. I later surmised that McDonalds' primary business is drive-through, and only about 10% of the population has their own car.

We decided to find the hotel and eat near the hotel or at the hotel if they had a restaurant. The hotel was surprisingly nice from the outside. It was a modern looking high-rise structure. My only fear was that we would have a room on a higher floor with no elevator, like the five-story hotel I had been living in. The driver dropped Marina and me off at the front door.

We were greeted at the front desk by a woman who spoke perfect English. I was surprised. After filling out paperwork and handing over our passports, we were given a key for the room and directions to its location. I had expected us to have more than one room, since there was three of us, but the woman at the desk informed us that the room was big enough for three adults.

Marina and I waited for Sergei in the lobby of the hotel. Sergei entered the lobby, and we boarded the elevator to go upstairs. We arrived on the proper floor and waited for the elevator doors to open. It seemed to take forever, and I thought, "That would be fitting, getting stuck in an elevator."

We walked down the hall to our room. Marina inserted the key in the lock, unlocked the door, and opened the door. I was surprised, but not really. There was a bedroom with a full-size bed, a bathroom, and a living room with a couch. I wondered how anyone could think that the room was big enough for three adults.

We discussed sleeping arrangements. Marina was insistent that I take the bed, but I refused.

"You will sleep in the bedroom, Sergei can have the couch, and I will sleep on the floor," I insisted. My reasoning was, as a gentleman, I should give the woman her privacy, and Sergei needed more sleep than I did. He had to drive back to Komsomolsk tomorrow.

Sergei agreed about Marina but said he would sleep on the floor. I would have no part of that, and as "the boss," I won the argument. After deciding on sleeping arrangements, Sergei said that he would go buy food and left for the store. When Sergei returned an hour later, we consumed the cheese, crackers, and canned mystery meet he had purchased and washed it down with vodka.

Sleep eluded me, and I tossed and turned all night. It was probably the wonderfully comfortable floor. Needless to say, the next morning, we arrived at the airport in time to catch my departing flight. My first rotation was complete once the wheels tucked away in the belly of the plane.

CHAPTER FIFTY-TWO

BACON IN YOUR POCKET?

The sun shined brightly across the green valley south of Pump Station 4 on the Trans-Alaska Pipeline. There was a slight breeze to keep the mosquitos away, and the crew was preparing to lift the new pipe into place.

Operations, HSE, management, and craft personnel were present at the pre-lift meeting. The pre-lift meeting, because of the lift over a live process line, is a standard operating procedure. During the pre-lift meeting, the lift plan is reviewed, any additional risks are identified, and each person on the team is assigned their specific responsibilities. Other lifts require a meeting but with much less formality.

Bob, one of the more experienced fitters on the crew, accepted the responsibility as the "signal man" on the ground, providing physical signals to the crane operator. Clarence, the operator, had performed many of these lifts and played along with the team in the meeting, but really had a lackadaisical attitude the entire meeting. Bob and Clarence would meet after the conclusion of the meeting to discuss the hand signals to be used during the lift.

The meeting droned on for about an hour, and at the conclusion, all sixteen people in the meeting felt confident a good plan was in place, and the lifting operation would go smoothly, without incident. The crew, along with the HSE guy, met at the work location. They had a final discussion about the lift and then began setting up barriers to ensure no one entered the lift zone.

Red "Danger" tape was strung between orange pylons, and doors into and out of the facility were barricaded with signs indicating imminent danger was present. It is a rare occurrence for a load to fall or a crane to topple, but every precaution is made to ensure personnel are kept out of harm's way.

Once the barrier was in place, the riggers began the process of inspecting and installing the lift straps around the eight-inch, twenty-five-foot piece of pipe. While the riggers installed the rigging, Clarence started the engine on the crane and began the process of pre-use checks to ensure the crane was functioning properly. He extended and retracted the outriggers, he extended and retracted the boom, he raised and lowered the boom, he rotated the crane three hundred and sixty degrees in both directions, and he raised and lowered the load hook.

Everything was good to go. The load hook was lowered, and the lifting eyes were placed in the cradle of the hook. The loaded hook was lifted just far enough to place tension in the rigging straps. Once tension was placed on the straps, the riggers left the exclusion zone, and Bob gave Clarence a big thumbs up, indicating the lift was a go.

The engine on the crane slightly revved as Clarence slowly began to lift the load. Bob stood by, watching the roofline of the building over which the load was to be lifted. He pointed his index finger skyward and slowly rotated it in a circular motion, indicating to Clarence to continue to lift. Once Bob was sure the load would clear the roof, he closed his hand in a fist, indicating not to lift any higher.

The crane was slowly rotated ninety-degrees, and the load was now suspended over the building, headed for its final destination. Bob signaled for Clarence to extend the boom, which would take the load out over the end of the building. The load hung there, over the end of the building, and Bob pointed to the ground and slowly rotated his index finger in a circular motion, the signal to lower the load.

Bob's eyes were affixed to the load to ensure adequate clearance from the building. He continued to slowly rotate his finger. What he didn't realize: something else had its eyes affixed on his finger. It was too late when Clarence realized what was about to happen. Out of nowhere, an arctic fox ran across the gravel pad and lunged towards Bob's outstretched arm.

The fox's razor-sharp teeth penetrated the lightweight glove that Bob was wearing. Bob yanked his hand away and swung at the fox. The damage was already done, and blood was already beginning to seep out of the glove. Clarence locked the crane into place and jumped down out of the cab, calling for security as he ran towards Bob.

"Pump 4 security, we need medical response ASAP. Bob just got bit by a fox," Clarence yelled into the radio. Within minutes, the medical response team was there. They removed Bob's glove and began to administer first aide. Security personnel also arrived and took a report from Clarence.

Security announced over the radio, "Attention all Pump

4 personnel, be on the lookout for an arctic fox on the pad. If spotted, do not approach. Notify security if spotted."

Bob was taken to the medical clinic within the facility where triage was performed. The EMT told Bob, "We will have to find the fox and verify that it is not rabid. If we are unable to find the fox quickly, we will transport you to Deadhorse to the medical clinic."

Bob just shook his head and thought, "Great. Just what I need, rabies."

A search was conducted for the next ninety minutes to try to locate the fox. Unfortunately, the little guy was never found. They are not big animals and probably average about five to ten pounds. It is estimated eighty percent of them are rabid.

Bob was driven the 150 miles to the medical clinic in Deadhorse. Because the animal was never found, Bob would have to undergo the vaccinations for rabies. This meant a series of thirteen shots in the stomach.

After receiving the shots and having the puncture wounds on his hand cleaned and bandaged, Bob was released by the doctor to return to work. He called over the radio in the clinic, "Pump 4 security, do you copy?"

After several attempts, a voice responded, "Go for Pump 4 security."

"This is Bob. I'm ready to leave the clinic."

Security responded, "Ten four. I'm in the parking lot in front of the clinic. I'll meet you at the entrance."

Bob thanked the medical staff and walked down the hallway to the entrance. As Bob exited the building, there at the entrance to the clinic, he was greeted by something unexpected, an arctic fox. The security guard sitting in the truck waiting for Bob honked, thus scaring the fox away.

The story spread across the vast North Slope about someone being attacked by an arctic fox. And as the story telling goes, additional embellishments are added to the story. Bob was ribbed by the team and told, "You would have never been attacked in the first place, or greeted at the clinic, if you weren't carrying bacon in your pocket."

CHAPTER FIFTY-THREE

COFFEE, TEA, OR M.E. (MATERIALS EXPEDITER)

A truly successful Alaskan story from a friend (Stephanie Leman) …

The summer of 1971 found me graduating from high school. I knew I would not be attending college; it just was not the path for me. I was beginning my adult life, on my own, and knew that I had to find a job. I had bills to pay. Therefore, I started looking for a permanent job.

I was fortunate to find a job. Reeve Aleutian Airways was hiring stewardesses. Yes, we were called stewardesses back then. Even though the fight for women's equality was well on its way, airlines still had not accepted anything other than young, attractive women to fill the roles as stewardesses. The term "flight attendant" would not come into being for many years.

I accepted a position as a stewardess and began flying to a multitude of locations on the Aleutian Chain, the islands that jut out from Alaska's mainland mass, stretching from the Kenai Peninsula to Attu, stretching 1,100 miles. I was fortunate to see many places, interesting places the general population will never see.

During the early 1970s, the United States had become economically stagnant. It was a recession. No different than the overall economy, I was stagnant. I was unable to save money, and times were lean. After listening to passengers talk about opportunities in the oil and gas industry, working on the North Slope, I decided it was time to hang-up my wings after four years.

A friend of mine was the business agent for the Teamsters, specifically the surveyors. He and I had several discussions about job opportunities, and after much consternation, I decided to make a career change in 1975. I joined the Teamsters Union, under his guidance and direction. He was a great mentor, and within no time, I received my first dispatch. I was dispatched to the North Slope, to a place called Happy Valley. Happy Valley was one of the construction camps along the Trans-Alaska Pipeline corridor. It is south of Prudhoe Bay. My job assignment was materials and warehousing. It was an exciting time. Construction was going full steam ahead on the Trans-Alaska Pipeline. I was young and eager to learn.

Thanks to a great man that I worked alongside of, I learned much about the oil and gas industry. He took me under his wing and taught me many things. One of the things I remember was hearing about a thing called a VSM. A VSM is a vertical support member. In most construction, these are referred to as piles, but, due to stringent requirements, they were given a special name to bypass some of the requirements (or so I'm told).

My friend made it his mission to educate me in all things pipelines, construction, and oil and gas. For the next two years, in his free time, he mentored me and set me up for success. I worked anywhere from two to six weeks before having time off.

I was transferred to the Chandalar Camp, which is near

Pump Station 4 of the Trans-Alaska Pipeline. The camp was south of Atigun Pass, on a "shelf." I continued to provide materials and warehouse support for the next two years, before being transferred to my final destination during the construction of the pipeline.

The final location I worked at was south of Prudhoe Bay: Franklin Bluffs. During my tenure at Franklin Bluffs Camp, we constructed Pump Station 2, which is about mile sixty of the pipeline. Another two years quickly passed, and it was time to transfer again.

I was moved to the Prudhoe Bay Construction Camp. Once the pipeline went into operation, I was moved into a permanent assignment in the Prudhoe Bay Materials/Warehouse Group. I spent the next twenty years working a rotation schedule in Prudhoe Bay when an exciting new opportunity opened. The Alpine field seventy-some miles west of Prudhoe Bay went into operation in 2000, and in 2001, I was asked if I was interested in transferring to Alpine.

I jumped at the opportunity to make the change. Little did I know that I would spend the next 18 years making new friends, reconnecting with old friends, and becoming an integral part of a team of great "can do" people.

I was fortunate to spend forty-four years working in the oil and gas industry in Alaska. I developed many lifelong friendships, met my husband, and became part of a wonderful team of people.

I have many fond memories of experiences and the amazing people that I met and worked with on the North Slope. I will always hold a special place in my heart for the people that I became friends with. I will always remember the events that brought us together like a family: softball games, special events with the locals in Nuiqsut, Wellness Challenges, Christmas gift exchanges, celebration dinners,

4th of July parades, Dash for Trash days, Friday Night Bingo, and so many other wonderful things that families do.

My spikies (special devices worn over boots or shoes to provide additional traction while walking on snow and ice) will never see another ice road. They are now hung up. But I will never forget the amazing people and experiences that I was afforded, working on the North Slope of Alaska.

ABOUT THE AUTHOR

I was welcomed into the world in Heidelberg, Germany. My father was enlisted in the United States Army, something he did for thirty-five years. I was the third child of six, one girl and five boys. I have no memories of Heidelberg other than 8mm family movies.

Growing up, I was fortunate to have lived in Texas, Kansas, Illinois, Hawaii, and Alaska. We were the typical military family, nomadic and always on the move. I attribute my ability to make friends easily to the military life. The longest we ever stayed in one place was four years.

My dad – August William Schuelke, Sr. – was born in Texas. Fort Hood, Texas was his home duty station and the place we rotated back to. My mom, Sylvia Dorothy Wirshels, was born in Chicago, Illinois. My parents met while dad was stationed in Chicago. They met one day while dad was driving a bus for a USO event. Dad told mom, "We're going to get married one day," while mom was entering the bus. They did get married soon after meeting and were together thirty-eight years before cancer took dad.

Dad ended his military career in Alaska, and it became home for the family. I had just graduated from high school in central Texas when we returned to Alaska for the second time. We settled into Delta Junction, a small town of about 2,500 people in the interior of the state.

There are several dichotomies in my familial roots. Dad

was born in the deep south of Texas; mom was born in the far north of Chicago. Dad's family immigrated from Germany in the 1800s; mom's parents immigrated from Lithuania in the early 1900s. I have always joked that my roots have created internal conflict: North vs. South, and Russia vs. Germany. In all honesty, it probably help set me up for success to deal with conflict.

I headed off to college in Fairbanks, one hundred miles north of Delta Junction. My original plan of becoming an architect changed because the university did not offer a program, and I could not afford to attend college out of state. I decided on civil engineering with an emphasis in structural engineering.

The cold temperatures of Fairbanks and a job opportunity in Anchorage caused me to transfer. I completed my degree program at the University of Alaska, Anchorage eleven years after starting. Except for my first two years of college, I went to school part-time and worked full-time, often working two jobs.

I was fortunate to work in many places and experience different things. I managed a couple of different restaurants and a Gold's Gym, worked in radio for a brief period, worked as a "bouncer" in several bars, worked for several small consulting firms as well as a large consulting firm, and eventually had a career in the oil industry.

My career in oil and gas was in construction management and lasted for twenty-five years. I was fortunate in my career to have stayed in Alaska for most of it. I worked on the international scene for a couple of years but realized that the international lifestyle was not for me.

My final job assignment, at my request, was in Houston, Texas. A little over a year after my relocation to Texas, the company made the decision to release me, no longer requiring my expertise in the current market.

Fortunately, because of my age and time in the industry, I was eligible for retirement benefits.

It has been a blessing. This book would not exist if I were still working, and it may have never come to fruition. In addition, my golf game would not be improving.

I owe this book to my family, my friends, and all the amazing people who influenced me throughout my life. I don't know if there will be a second volume, but the amazing stories in the oil and gas industry are endless.

Thank you!

John

Find me at johnjschuelke.com where you will see the progress of other books I have planned.

Made in the USA
Columbia, SC
16 May 2023

16830352R00126